A true story…in her own words how a

SECOND OPINION

saved my wife's life from third stage cancer

BY

JACK FORSBERG

the Peppertree Press
Sarasota, Florida

Copyright © Jack Forsberg, 2015
All rights reserved. Published by the Peppertree Press, LLC.
the Peppertree Press and associated logos are trademarks of
the Peppertree Press, LLC.
No part of this publication may be reproduced, stored in a retrieval system,
transmitted in any form or by any means, electronic, mechanical, photocopying,
recording, or otherwise, without prior written permission of the publisher and
author/illustrator. Graphic design by Rebecca Barbier.

For information regarding permission,
call 941-922-2662 or contact us at our website:
www.peppertreepublishing.com or write to:
the Peppertree Press, LLC.
Attention: Publisher
1269 First Street, Suite 7
Sarasota, Florida 34236

ISBN: 978-1-61493-361-8

Library of Congress Number: 2015940009

Printed September 2015

An Overview

This book is composed so that you can follow a sequence of events based on Midge's and Jack's Journals. Starting from the time Midge first learns she has cancer until her cancer is put into remission. You need to keep in mind that she is a person dealing with the multiple stages of lung cancer… a deadly, life threatening disease. For this reason she is at times very emotional, so please excuse the grammatical errors as she is merely writing down her thoughts as they come to her during this high stress period of her life.

Midge's Journal

From the time I first discovered cancer I decided to keep an on-going journal about the experience. I needed something solid I could refer to during all my ups and downs of the different treatments. From my own, Jack's, and my children's research. I felt I was well informed. I was at times a book-keeper and then comptroller for our ad agency for forty years so I knew how to keep good records.

Jack's Journal

I decided to do my journal to use as a reference source for all the medical tests Midge needed as well as the doctor's advice. As I got into it I realized …as Midge did that this was also a place for us to unload some of our frustrations.., such as lost tests that were critical to Midge's recovery.

Midge

Dedication

    This book is dedicated to Midge Forsberg who was my love, companion and best friend for fifty years as well as a great mother for our four children. She was also a bookkeeper and later comptroller for our Ad Agency for forty years. She was always up on the latest news and enjoyed comparing facts with what the politicians had to say. She was also a good medical researcher on treatment options. In the years after she put cancer into remisssion, she edited and published four books, three for me and one large, life-time poetry book for my brother.

Contents

CHAPTER ONE	Original Diagnosis	1
CHAPTER TWO	First Opinion	10
CHAPTER THREE	Insurance Problems	17
CHAPTER FOUR	Second Opinion	22
CHAPTER FIVE	Third Opinion	27
CHAPTER SIX	Fourth Opinion	33
CHAPTER SEVEN	Proton & Chemo	40
CHAPTER EIGHT	Bad Day At Flat Rock	47
CHAPTER NINE	My Son's Visit	54
CHAPTER TEN	Cancer Results, Proton & Chemo	58
CHAPTER ELEVEN	Bedside Mystery Over	63
CHAPTER TWELVE	Finding A Miracle	68
CHAPTER THIRTEEN	Midge's "Bucket List"	74
CHAPTER FOURTEEN	Bone Cancer	83
CHAPTER FIFTEEN	Major Breathing Problems	89
CHAPTER SIXTEEN	Poems & Memories	95
	The Morning After	95
	The Journey Alone	97
	God's Special Angels	99
	The Chaplain	102

Let Her Live Lord	104
The Stone	105
Memories	107
Love	109
My Cancer	111
To Understand God's Love	113
The Exchange	114
The Anniversary	115
Leave It Behind	117
The Vatican	119
Song Of The Loons	121
Midge	123

Chapter One

Original Diagnosis

Jack's Journal

THE FIRST SIGNS

We were in the middle of our fall color tour around Wisconsin and the UP in Michigan. This fall color trip was one we especially enjoyed. Midge was driving just south of Escanaba when she suddenly felt faint. She had never had spells like this before so we were both concerned. As soon as we got home, we went to Midge's regular doctor and she ordered some tests. Midge said she felt like she was coming down with a chest cold so her doctor also ordered X-rays of her lungs just to be safe.

A few days later her doctor called and asked if Midge could come in for a PET scan to get a better reading on what they saw on the x-rays.

After the PET scan her doctor sent us to see a cancer doctor to show us the results of her PET scan and what he had discovered. His office was in the Sparrow Hospital building in Lansing, Michigan. Midge, my son John and I went up to see what they had found. It was very clear there was a mass in the top right lung about the size of a quarter..Plus, they found a small lump at the top of her trachea. He explained they would not know for sure what it was until they did a biopsy. It very well could be cancer but they had to have that confirmed by having a small part of it examined in the lab.

Midge's Journal

CANCER: DAY ONE—OCTOBER 9, 2009

Well today was the 'big day' that I learned that I probably have lung cancer. The doctor showed me their Pet Scan and they found a one inch round tumor with some stuff' surrounding it that does NOT look good. The surgeon will set up time for a biopsy surgery. I can only hope he is a miracle worker. This is NOT a good situation and I guess I need to make some plans. There is a good chance it is cancer.

8 PM

After getting the news from the surgeon we went to dinner at the Airport Bar and I shared an 8 oz Fillet with Jack plus a glass of Lombroso wine. We had a good laugh about how years ago we always went to celebrate when we paid off a bank loan. Seemed like a good reason to have dinner and a drink back then too. We knew this was going to be the beginning of a long and bad trip for both of us. So we better celebrate now while we still can.

9 AM NEXT MORNING

My mind is racing in all directions at the moment and I can't seem to focus on one thing I need to do right now. I should call Steve in Las Vegas….he is the only one of the kids that knows I have been taking tests….I will have to tell him that they found something but then I probably need to tell the others….But once I start telling everyone then it is for sure that this is really happening. What I have to try to do is 'not panic' which I feel I am on the verge of at this moment. God this is going to be a journey I am NOT going to like.

I guess we have decided to go up north to the cabin this morning for the week-end and stay till mid week unless they get me into the specialist sooner (not likely). It is going to be a pretty good test to see if I can act like all is well with the Tustin folks at the church....but I really don't want any of our Tustin friends to know this until I have the biopsy and a prognosis for my future (if I have one). I am always such a pessimist but of course I am hoping they can do something....but at the same time I pretty much think that they can't stop the process. Not sure if this writing about it is going to help or hurt my dealing with this but thought I would like to at least start. Want to write some things to the kids and Jack but that will come later. Right now I am just feeling overwhelmed.

OUR LOG CABIN ON THE PINE RIVER—SATURDAY AM

Well, I have now talked to Steve and told him my condition and I knew he would be upset. I had already told him I was going in for tests so I had to tell him the results. Steve wanted details of course.

He was really concerned and wants to come home but I said no, not just yet. Let's get some more tests behind me. But I do want him to come home too. I then talked to Peggy and that was upsetting for both of us. Sort of wish I had not dumped on her tonight, she has a lot of other stuff to worry about.

Midge's Journal

STARTING A STRATEGY

I had a good talk with John and Morgan. They both know people that have this and are still around five years etc... That was very good to hear. He then talked to Jack privately (my suggestion) and after they talked Jack came in here and told me that after they establish that it is cancer and before we allow any surgery we need to do some research, etc. John is having Morgan, his wife do some for us too and that is very good. Of course he told me I have to keep a 'positive attitude' and I will try (really) but right at the present it seems very difficult. More like impossible with what I know. This has been a very long day so I think I will go to bed. I know I will have trouble sleeping. This is going to be a tough road to travel for both me and Jack.

SETTING AN APPOINTMENT—WEDNESDAY MORNING

The doctor's scheduler set up my first appointment for Wednesday, October 21 at 8 am. Well now I know one thing I will be doing on our anniversary. Jack will run in to get the paperwork so I can have it filled out before I go into surgery. They were going to put it in the mail but as we are going to the cabin.....plus there is also a chance it wouldn't be here by Tuesday either. We decided we would pick it up and drop off the discs.

The weekend through Tuesday went pretty good. Got home to Grand Ledge from our cabin late in the afternoon after stopping at the Mt. Pleasant casino and having lunch with Ardyth and Jim. I filled them in on what we know now before surgery.

GOT TO GET POSITIVE

Peggy called me to tell me that in her talks with John last night, he was a lot more positive and said that with Morgan's dad, they did not even do a biopsy. But of course the surgeon could not know for sure on my CT scan and it was only my regular doctor that said he had to do a biopsy.…(boy leave it to me to always find the 'dark' side of anything). Gotta work on this positive stuff a bit more for sure! Anyway, Peggy said John also told her that there are several different cancers and some are very treatable and we just have to wait and see, so I will try to set my sights on that for now.

LOT OF THINGS ON MY MIND JACK'S GOING TO NEED HELP

It was a VERY long night last night and I had so many nutty thoughts….things I had to do before I can't…..one was even to get down there and finish painting the basement door and wall…Like ANYONE cares about that….I do have to get some things organized for Jack. I thought of all the bill paying, assets to keep tabs on and all that stuff…he doesn't HAVE A CLUE how to do any of that right now. Hope I can get all that shaped up for him and then maybe get Sue to pay bills for him. Most regular bills I have set to AUTO pay now and I will set up all the others that I can….then make a list of annual things like taxes, homeowners insurance and that stuff that require checks. Oh boy, that is going to be something Jack will not want to do so hopefully we can work something out with Sue on that stuff.

SOME GOOD NEWS

Our anniversary is coming up and I'm sure we won't be doing anything special for that. I don't think we had anything planned anyway, but everything is going to hinge on how my tests turn out. It doesn't look good. I just got a phone call from my regular doctor that my CT scan came back OK and I said WHAT....and she said the CT we.had done...so I said "well the lung was not so good... so one out of two is OK. She said Oh,, this one was for your head. I am a little more relaxed today and a bit calmer now than I SHOULD be...don't know if I am getting used to this (NOT) or if the family telling me it will all work out. It has been a bit easier not to talk or think about it. That has helped for now anyway.

OUR ANNIVERSARY 10 AM—OCTOBER 21, 2009

We are off to the doctor this morning and it is also our anniversary. Should be quite an epic day. I took two Benadryl last night and slept pretty good. Woke up just before the alarm went off at 6 AM. It is our anniversary and I know Jack feels really terrible that this thing is happening to us. I am still so confused I don't know what to think right now. Maybe later when things calm down a bit. I don't like the nights though….. those damn panic attacks leave me breathless and sweaty.

9 PM

Well it does not look good from what I heard today. The Surgeon is doing the biopsy next Thursday (if I pass the heart stress test…wouldn't want to die of a heart attack when they are doing surgery). What the surgeon says is….IF the lymph nodes are infected (they do not look good) then that is ALL he would do and I would go home that day. If they are NOT infected (not likely) then he would remove the lung mass and that would take several hours and I would be in the hospital for a week or so. Didn't hear much good news that's for sure. I can hardly believe this is happening.. It is almost like a bad dream that really isn't true but it may come true very soon. It all hinges on the biopsy. I just hope I can take it.

Jack's Journal

OCTOBER 22—10 AM

We have managed to get through our anniversary with the very worst news of our entire lives. Instead of celebrating nearly fifty good years of life together, we are going to be facing the very worst trauma I can imagine.. We spent part of the day at the doctor's office and I didn't hear any good news at all and neither did Midge. damn, damn damn. I do have to find something positive; some way to go ahead with a cancer treatment we can both agree on… before it gets worse. Everything hinges on the biopsy.

Midge's Journal

OCTOBER 22

I feel a bit overwhelmed. Tomorrow I need to get a TO DO list going because Jack is going to need a lot of help knowing what to do in a lot of areas. He has always let me do all the bill paying plus about anything to do with the house and cabin, so I need to get some things in place for him. There are a lot of things he needs to know.

FRIDAY—OCTOBER 23, 2009

Ready to go for the heart stress test. Hope my knee holds out long enough. Also had a rough time sleeping last night and really feel tired today. God what else? Gotta get some kind of a handle on trying to be positive as I know this is going to be a long, drawn out thing. I've seen too many friends go thru this. Well at least the stress test is no big thing so I don't expect any bad news there (I hope). At least I will know how my heart is doing, or not doing depending how this effects my heart. I'll just wait and see on that.

HEART STRESS TEST—9 PM

The stress test was not very stressful….but it was long. Took about three hours total. I did not get on a treadmill so that was good because my knee probably would not have liked that. They increased my heart rate to over 120 (I think the goal was 124?) by using chemicals, but it worked. It was a weird feeling but my heart was really going fast and you could really feel it. Wasn't scary though, just weird.

I am pretty sure that it all went well and don't expect any problem with my heart at least. We went to dinner at the Old Demarco's on Pennsylvania (don't know the name of it now). Had a glass of wine (they said I could) and a great deep dish pizza that we have had before. We are settled in for the night with TV and I really hope to get some rest tonight. Seems like my spirits are like a yo-yo and they are always down in the middle of the night. I can do without the panic attacks.

I wake up and my mind is racing all over the place.

I really need some good rest tonight.

Jack's Journal

OPERATION OR BIOPSY? —OCT. 24

The last few days have been finger biting time for the whole family due to the worst news of our lives. Finally the day HAS arrived for the surgery… or the biopsy. The whole family is here. John, Peggy, Don and me, even including my brother Terry all except (Steve in Vegas who is waiting to hear) The doctor has made it very clear that if it is only in the lung he would do major surgery to remove the mass..

But, if it has spread to the lymph glands which means it is in Midge's blood, he would just do the biopsy only. Naturally we are hoping for surgery. It would be tougher, but then it would be over. Major surgery would take at least three or four hours. **The doctor was out in an hour and twenty minutes.**

NO GOOD NEWS

We all knew it did not go well, It is probably in the lymph glands. Damn. Damn, Damn. The nurse guided us to a small waiting room to wait for the doctor to give us his opinion. This will not be good news.

Chapter Two

First Opinion

Your love's the only anchor
on this fragile ship of life
so I pray that you hear me
as I'm pleading for my wife

Jack's Journal

THE FIRST OPINION: SPARROW HOSPITAL—OCT. 24, 2009

The doctor came in and explained that he always presented his findings to the family as the patient was always under sedation and usually didn't remember what he said. He was very blunt.

He said it was now third stage lung cancer and it had already entered her lymph glands and it was very difficult to treat.

He said "You have very few options. I imagine you will contact some oncologists and I have never met one that didn't insist on chemotherapy. I don't agree with that. I feel she might rather go home, get her things in order, and enjoy the time she has left. From my experience that will be about six months or so and you will only gain about six weeks more with chemo therapy and she will be very sick most of the time. But that is your decision.' He left the room.

WE SAT THERE SHELL SHOCKED

I am sure every one of us went somewhere and broke down and cried. It was so utterly final. Literally a brutal death sentence for Midge. Now there was no doubt that Midge had a very serious cancer and there was a chance she would not survive it. I was hoping and praying they would discover it was not that serious…instead of this.

At this point our feelings toward her surgeon was that he was the most cold hearted doctor we had ever run into. Also somehow the doctors opinion had gotten to Midge that the ensuing pain would not be worth the little extra time she had to live. We had to somehow convince her otherwise… by finding a different opinion. One that was more positive with proven results that she could really believe. We felt her first instinct would be to trust what the doctor said and try to follow it. We were right. She was adamant she would do what he had advised us. We knew we had to find some answers fast to change her mind…a more positive opinion.

Midge's Journal

OCT. 24, 9 PM

Well so much for this surgeon being my savior or miracle worker. He just told my family the blunt truth…no sugar coating in his speech. As my Dad would have said 'he just tells it like he sees it."

Of course the whole family feels he over did it but that is only how he sees to treat it…..and that don't look good. He must have read my mind on chemo. I have always dreaded it. Mostly due to the fact it just about destroys you before it helps, and then the pain and you go bald. Wow. I can hardly take a deep breath. Didn't expect to get quite this much bottom line dumped on me. The truth hurts.

I feel bad for Steve. He's been calling about every day and now he wants some good news. I think I should call him but need to get over this shock first. He will be devastated. I feel like I am his safety net or life line. Jack will try to fill that but don't know how that will go. I think I will have John call him first. Gotta start sorting this out,…it's still a shock…never quite expected my end to be this soon.

Midge's Journal

FRIENDS AND RELATIVES

Busy week-end. We went to Battle Creek casino with Terry and Judy on Saturday. Gone most of the day. Had a good time. Tried not to think about it today. I won a bit of money even. Had a great dinner at Shulers in Marshall, Michigan (where we went on our honeymoon). Talked with Judy and Terry about myself a bit but kept it pretty light. I did not mention my night fears or other problems.

Sunday was Jack's birthday party in Williamston and it was great. I didn't do much of anything there but Peggy and Morgan served the cake and that was good. John and Morgan did the poem presentation for Jack that was just incredible. They did it so well. Terry wrote a very nice poem for Jack too, like he always does on these occasions. It was beautiful.

Midge's Journal

NIGHT SWEATS

I was able to get through those two days very well, but the nights still get to me a bit....wake up at 3 or 4 am and my mind just starts racing in all directions and I cannot sleep. Should have gotten that melatonin. Steve says it really works. Peggy told us about that sleep aid that Lindsay found and it really works. Maybe I will ask the doctor tomorrow if it is okay for me to use. I really need to get some good sleep. Hope this night panic don't last.

OCTOBER 26, 2009—10 PM

Got my hair colored today and told Cindy about me… just a very abbreviated version. She was good and didn't press, but she even got tears in her eyes so she left to go mix some dye and was fine when she came back We talked that if things go okay I may get a perm 'next time' to see if that makes doing my hair easier. Color usually helps too. Jack went golfing with T.A. and Jim while I got my hair done. It is his birthday today and I totally forgot to even say happy birthday. Went to Penney's after my hair coloring and just got him some "mom" type stuff that he needs and never buys for himself boxer shorts, shirts, and a new pair of Docker pants. Not much for his 75th but he liked them. Birthdays don't seem quite so important now…. although I hope I have a few more left.

Midges Journal

OCTOBER 28, 2009

Don't feel good at all tonight and my voice is so bad. I imagine that is one of my first symptoms and when the symptoms really start taking effect I bet I will be REALLY anxious then. So far outside of my voice, there is nothing really. The thing in my leg may have a connection to all this if it has spread....but outside of that and my voice, nothing except I don't FEEL good. Trying not to dwell....but doesn't seem to work at night. Enough already! The nights are always the worst....too many things going on.

NOVEMBER 1, 2009 **SUNDAY MORNING**

Ups and downs, that is all I have been experiencing for the past week and it has really been mostly downs! I have GOT to break out of this and get a bit of spark because I sure don't want it to go like this for however long it is for crying out loud! Why is it always so much worse in the middle of the night. Good grief I was going to die sometime....and I guess knowing that it is coming on strong should make me want to do everything I can do before I get where I can't do anything. How come I don't know what the devil I want to do. Jack keeps asking me and is being so good about trying to keep me doing things....maybe this is just one of the steps I have to go through on this journey. (I hope it doesn't last long, but then watch out what you wish for) Hope the next phase is a bit more reflective and calming. I hate these middle of the night panic things. Jim just called and he and Ardyth would like to do something with us this afternoon and I think we will. They have been good friends for a long time and Jack will want to lean on them too I know...so hopefully Jim doesn't give me a 'time line' I don't think he will. He worked in nursing homes and saw a lot of this type of thing.

Jack's Journal

NOVEMBER 2, 2009

Ardyth is my first cousin and we grew up together like sister and brother. We have been like that our entire lives so now we always keep track of what is going on with each other. Jim is her husband and one of my best friends. We all hunt together at the old farm house of Ardyth's parents…my uncle and aunt. We also go to the casino's together and meet for lunch whenever we can to catch up on things. We will be meeting them to fill them in as soon as we can on this whole thing with Midge. I am sure they are praying for Midge as much as I am. Actually the entire Lutheran church in Tustin will be praying for Midge because that is the kind of people they are.

Jim was in nursing home management for a long time and he has seen a lot of this type of thing. He will probably give us some advice on that if I know Jim. I don't think Midge wants to hear any bad news though right now

Midge's Journal

SUNDAY AM

We are now at our house on the Looking Glass River in Michigan. Better get ready and meet Jack for breakfast.

He wanted me to go to church in Grand Ledge but I never have in the past so it seems a bit hypocritical to go because I have this going on. I do want prayers for strength to see this through without blowing it though. I like our little church in Tustin and I do have many friends there that I am sure of,.. as each calls or sends me a card. They will pray for me.

NOV. 9, 2009

We went north to our log cabin on the Pine river near Tustin for the weekend. A short trip...went late Friday after doing a full body scan and bone scan at MMP in East Lansing, Michigan. We went to church in Tustin Sunday and I was a bit surprised how few of my friends knew about it. I thought Pat Otberg and George Klinger would have told others (was hoping so I would not have to) but I guess they thought I would rather they did not because it ended up that I had to talk A LOT about it and that is up setting. Everyone was very nice though so that was good. We went to breakfast with Pat Otberg and afterward Jack went to see Elna at the nursing home. She is a neighbor and friend and friend of his folks. One GOOD thing happened on the way home to our home in Grand Ledge, Stopped at the Soaring Eagle Casino in Mt. Pleasant and I won over $1,200 profit. Not bad. Hope that is not all my good luck though.

Chapter Three

Insurance Problems

Midge's Journal

MAJOR INSURANCE PROBLEM—NOV. 11

We are now in our home on the Looking Glass River near Grand Ledge, Michigan. Today we found that we cannot go to MDA or probably any other out of state cancer center because of our #$% Blue Cross/Blue Shield insurance. John did the research He called the Houston Cancer Hospital in Texas and Sloan Kettering in New York, and both said "No" we do not accept Blue Cross/ Blue Shield Insurance, period, end of story. I went spastic, so I called Blue Cross/Blue Shield and they said "Sorry, we give each health care provider a chance to accept our card and if they refuse to accept it there is nothing we can do.. That is their decision, period. I have an idea it is because of their slow pay. I was frantically fighting for time and I didn't need this to happen. I also had to be sure that switching Insurance companies would not jeopardise my medical coverage.

Jack's Journal ... Same day

FINDING MEDICAL INSURANCE

Nothing was more important at this time than having the right medical insurance for Midge. Her medical records were still getting lost and this was also very critical to her being accepted by a cancer hospital. We were both under pressure and we also knew timing was critical to start Midge's cancer treatments. In essence we were being told you are just not that important to us. I called my brother Terry and told him we had just been turned down by two of the best cancer hospitals in the country due to our insurance company. He found that unbelievable. I agreed.

WE DO NOT ACCEPT CASH

My brother suggested I tell them we would cover the cost no matter how they wanted it … they could set up a bond and they could take it out of that or we could pay cash … whatever they wanted.

They said, "No, that does not work in our system.. You must have an acceptable credit card. We started searching for a good, southern insurance company that was respected all over the south.

We called several firms and interviewed them over the phone with the idea that they must be accepted for the hospital's we were going to visit. One name kept coming up. It was Humana Insurance. That seemed to be a favorite in the south.

Midge's Journal

NEW INSURANCE, NEW CREDIT CARD—NOV. 13

We found a Humana representative and after going over all the details, we decided to go with them. We found they were very popular in the south. We set up with them for both Jack and my insurance starting Jan. 1, 2010. We had to keep Blue Cross/Blue Shield until the end of the year. Being over 65 we had our Medicare card and now with the Humana Supplement card I would be accepted wherever we went. They assured us all of our Prescriptions were covered by Humana. We went in to get a prescription called "Caduet" that was one of Jack's standard drugs. They said Humana does not cover Caduet. We finally got that worked out.

Putting all this together at one time over a few days left both of us pretty stressed out. We were literally fighting for my life and we knew it. One step forward and two steps back. We still needed to get my medical records transferred. We got all my reports and scans sent to U of M though and should have an appointment at least in a few days. Our contact said we probably will have an appointment on Friday. Hope John can go with us. He is a cool head and knows a lot about this stuff. He and Morgan have been doing their medical research for me. They are both very good at this type of thing and will keep us up to date on what they find. I am still very uneasy about chemo .and really don't want to go that route unless there is VERY clear evidence that I have a good chance of some extra years of good health.

Midge's Journal

SOME GOOD NEWS—NOV. 14

One good thing we heard today…**the bone and full body scans were negative** and that is the very first thing I've heard that may be hopeful. At least it is not in my bones, or not now anyway. Not sure about the lymph nodes though…that is probably another matter. Oh well, will probably get all that news in Ann Arbor Hospital. We sent all my tests down there and we have an appointment to meet their oncologists. I don't expect any good news.

Jack's Journal

UNIVERSITY OF MICHIGAN HOSPITAL—NOV. 15

At last John, Peggy, Midge and I met with the Oncologists at Ann Arbor Hospital. He would be the one Midge would be working with if we decided on the U of M Hospital. The Dr. was very thorough and treated us well explaining all their programs. The cancer trials they were offering sounded very promising. Not without some pain and discomfort but that it could be cured. He did not mention proton therapy. He did mention radiation treatments and chemo…a combination of the two.

We left feeling a bit more positive. He spent alot of time explaining all their treatment programs and what he would recommend. Chemo was still at the center of a cure for the cancer in the lymph glands. He said he could get Midge into one of their best trial treatment programs.

QUESTIONS TO ASK YOUR DOCTOR OR HOSPITAL ONCOLOGIST
FROM MY *TEST RESULTS* CAN YOU TELL ME*

1. What type of cancer do I have?
   Is it a virus, a bacteria, is it hereditary or could it be caused from the environment? Is it fast growth or slow growth?

2. What are my options for tTreatment?
   chemo, radiation, surgery or what other?

3. For my type of cancer, are there proven methods of treatment that can put it into remission?

4. Are you associated with test trial programs or are you affiliated with cancer research centers?

5. If I agree to have chemo, how effective are the drugs to prevent nausea and hair loss? How long would the chemo normally take to put my cancer into remission? Times for other treatments?

6. Are you aware of another facility that might be a better fit for curing my type of cancer? Would you advise a second opinion at this point?

7. There are so many unknown factors. Could you just offer me the ultimate known and tested program available?

8. What is most beneficial...to increase my activity, moderate or more rest? Is there anything I should be very concerned about, or to avoid before treatment?.

Chapter Four

Second Opinion

Midge's Journal

SECOND OPINION—NOV. 16
UNIVERSITY OF MICHIGAN HOSPITAL, ANN ARBOR, MICHIGAN

We had our second major meeting in Ann Arbor this morning and it went as I thought. The Oncologists only wanted to do chemo, therapy plus radiation. I found out I am 3B stage (not good at all) and that is because it is in both the lung and the lymph nodes. Chemo is the only thing to slow it down. The meeting went as good as could be expected, No magic treatment without pain. He was more positive but I don't feel like I have much hope of stopping this really. Jack and John and Peggy came up with a good series of questions for the U of M Hospital oncologist and I felt that he answered them all including trials. No good news though. Both Jack and John keep saying we need a few more options for treatment preferably down south where there is a warmer climate. That sounds better if I have to do it. At least it will be warmer. We have a condo that we always lease for a few months in Bradenton, Florida and there are several large hospitals in that area.

THINKING HOW I MUST FACE IT ALONE—NOV. 17

We talked about doing the chemo (if I do) in Florida and that is what I would like to do.... I THINK.....the kids all have their lives going good. I am not going to be fun to be around and as John and Peggy agreed...being in a nice new condo with not having to worry about house work, etc., should help me a lot. I think if I get very bad though I am going to be sorry not to have my family around me. They can come and visit of course but then...I have to do this alone and that I know is how everyone goes out. Jack will be good I am sure ...but no one can ease the fear but me. I do well with it most of the time, but then it comes back. We are all going to die and I know that...guess I have had a good run (as I like to say) but yet you still want to hang on. Why, I am not sure. I think most of my fear has to do with how painful, or how bad this is all going to get before the end. I hope they can keep me from falling into despair and making everyone miserable around me. Wow, what am I thinking. Well tonight...sort of wish it was over I think. Tomorrow will be a better day.....maybe.

RESEARCHING PROTON TREATMENT—NOV. 18

I was actually looking for Cancer Centers and their special treatments for Lung cancer. I came across this new treatment for prostate cancer in Loumi, CA. The same one Jack's friend from high school in Michigan used for putting his prostate cancer into remission.

Once I started reading about it, I was fascinated. I am familiar with the laser beam and how it works but this was a much finer beam, much more intense and could be precisely controlled. My first thought was...is it dangerous or could it work on a tiny spot of cancer in my lung without hitting my voice box?

It is a huge machine, like a cyclotron in stages. It generates a very concise beam that can be minutely controlled and then turned off instantly so there is no damage beyond the target area..It is very expensive to build and house the machine. It cost over one hundred and fifty million to build and there are about four in operation and eleven in various stages of planning or construction. If all the things I am reading about it are true, it may be something we should check out for me. I like the idea that it is very precise and doesn't hurt any other part of your body. I found there is one in Jacksonville Florida, five hours from our condo in Florida. We will check that out.

When we get to Florida we will call and get their opinion of what proton could do for me.

Jack's Journal

A NEW CANCER TREATMENT? —NOV. 20

Midge said she just found more information on-line about the proton treatment we first heard of in church. Our church in Tustin is always a good place to get medical news on people in the area so when I was at church, I talked to Devere Byers. His sister Verna who I went to school with in Tustin, Michigan now lives in Alaska and her husband Gary just recovered from cancer.. He had a treatment called 'Proton" that sends a very fine beam to the cancer and dissipates it over a period of time. I called Verna and Gary Eley in Alaska and they gave me a lot of information on the proton treatment therapy. Gary had prostate cancer and he went for treatments in Loumi, CA and they put his cancer into remission with no side effects. He said patients were taking a treatment in the morning and playing golf in the afternoon. Gary just couldn't say enough good about proton therapy.

Midge researched it on line and then talked to a doctor at the Center. She let him know we were interested and were going to be in Jacksonville Florida soon....within two weeks. When she talked to the doctor again, she found out his specialty was proton therapy at the Center and he said he would need all of Midge's tests and then a team of doctors would decide if she was right for their treatments and he would get back to her. She said he sounded like it would all depend on her test reports.

Jack's Journal

STARTING SOUTH TO FLORIDA—NOV. 24. 2009

By the time we packed and left for Florida, we needed a break to unwind from all the stress of tests and fighting to get our insurance credit cards in order.

We would be on the road three days and my brother Terry and Judy had already left for Florida and had found a great country musical in Kentucky. They wanted us to see it. It was in Renfu Valley Kentucky and we made a point to find it and go to the play. It was country at its funniest. We got front row seats and we laughed until it hurt. There were about 30 in the cast and they were very talented. They could all play a number of instruments and dance. They had the whole crowd roaring at their wild antics. It was a great stop for us. We found out it was a show they put on just before Christmas every year. It had been going on for years. We met some folks that were there year after year. They had ten curtain calls of standing ovations.

On our way to Florida we called Moffit Cancer Hospital in Tampa and told them we were coming. They said yes, they would accept our new Humana credit card. We sent all the reports and scans from Lansing and the U of M to Moffit. We set up a time to meet and consult with them We knew Moffit was in Tampa, just one hour from our condo in Bradenton,

Florida, so it would be easy for us to go back and forth for treatments if we selected Moffit Cancer Hospital

Jack's Journal

OUR CONDO IN BRADENTON—NOV. 28

We reached Bradenton at night and unpacked at our condo in Pinebrook Circle. It is a beautiful condo on the fourth floor overlooking a lake and golf course. We had sent a cashiers check for three months in advance, just before we found Midge had cancer.

We immediately started planning for our visit to Moffit Hospital and also to the Proton Therapy Center in Jacksonville... the latter being five and half hours north of us. We wanted to check out both places before we made a decision. We wanted to be sure our records were sent to Moffit. Again we found out some of them didn't make it. After several days of checking with East Lansing, U of M and Moffit, we finally got the records transferred. There were a lot of checking, and phone calls that drove both of us up a wall. As it all takes time we didn't have. We wanted to get a therapy program for Midge started as soon as possible.

After talking to Gary Eley in Alaska, Midge said she had been on line and found more about the proton centers in the US as well as the one in Jacksonville, Florida. Each of *their* facilities cost over 150 million dollars and are very complex. We found they are using it for other cancers now besides prostate so we want to go there after we meet with Moffit Hospital.

Chapter Five

Third Opinion

Midge's Journal

MEETING WITH MOFFIT HOSPITAL—DEC. 7. 2009

We had called Moffit Hospital earlier and talked to one of their Oncologists and they said yes, they would accept our Humana Insurance Card. We went up to Moffit and met their Oncology doctor. She was very nice, upbeat and very professional. She explained their program in detail and said I could get into one of their trials and she felt very strongly it would be successful. We left feeling this was going to be an excellent alternative if we did not go with the Proton Treatment. The doctor said we could even combine the proton from Jacksonville with their chemo and therapy program here at Moffit for my treatments. I was very impressed by her. She was very positive ,but was she accurate? My negative attitude popping up again. We found there were people in our condo complex that had gone through cancer treatments at Moffit and they came out with their cancer in remission which was very good news.

Midge's Journal

JACKSONVILLE, FLORIDA—DEC. 9

After we left the Moffit Cancer Hospital we drove up to The Proton Center in Jacksonville and they had arranged for us to stay in the Best Western Motel near the airport.. This was until we got through the tests to see if they felt I would be accepted into the program.

We had a pool, a workout room and a nice motel room about ten miles from the proton center.

A PROTON/ CHEMO CANCER PATIENT DECISION TIME —DEC. 10, 2009

I also knew that now we had to make a decision. Right after we arrived the doctor I talked to left me a name of a patient that had gone through the proton and chemo program recently. I talked to her for over an hour and she really filled me on a lot of the details. It was an awakening for me. .I got first hand what was to happen to me and the end results. She was very frank and I appreciated that. .When she got through all of it, I felt I really understood what I was in for and how it would turn out. She didn't sugar coat the problems with chemo and that was my big fear. She said the proton was no problem, just uncomfortable. But they would give me some help with the meds to offset some of the chemo problems. But she was now in remission and felt it really worked… so that was the bottom line. How long…who knew?? I thanked her profusely. I would say she made the decision for us.

It did a great deal of good for my attitude too. Now I felt much more positive about the treatments.

Overview (by Jack)

WHY LOST TEST RESULTS ARE CRITICAL

The one thing we found that happened every time we went from one medical faculty to another was the loss of Midge's test results. This may seem trivial but if even just a few of the test records were missing it was a big problem. The doctors at the next medical facility or hospital had **to have every test result** before they would accept Midge for an appointment.

They also needed to know the result of each test as this is the only way they could analyze Midge for a particular treatment. Also a progression of test records told them how or if the cancer was growing. From these test results they could also suggest what treatments they would recommend. For example; radiation, chemo, surgery or some other treatment.

The test records were also very important if she suffered from certain allergies, or other health problems. Plus for Midge it always delayed our appointments and cost us time. As you can imagine we wanted Midge into the best treatment program as fast as possible to start healing the cancer or putting it into remission.

Jack's Journal

DEC. 11, 2009

We will be staying at the Best Western motel here in Jacksonville until all the tests are finished and they make a decision on how to treat Midge. We have a nice pool and a work-out room. It is about ten miles from the Proton Center and traffic is frantic in the AM. Once we know what Midge's schedule will be… then hopefully we can find a more permanent place.

Midge's Journal

QUALIFYING FOR PROTON THERAPY—DEC. 12

I had all of our records from the U of M, Lansing and Moffit sent to the Proton Center in Jacksonville. The pathology slides and the doctors notes on the PET scan did not make it. Again this cost us another few days waiting for the transfers to be made of all the tests before we could meet with the proton doctor. Finally after several days they had most of Midge's records and called us for a meeting with the proton doctor.

Midges Journal

MEETING THE PROTON DOCTOR—DEC, 14

We drove into Jacksonville and we met Dr. Hoppe, the Proton Specialist.. He was young professional and very positive. He answered all our questions and explained what would be required prior to proton. I had to have a body cast that would be my bed for all the treatments. I would have to be precisely measured with X's on my body that would be there all through the treatments. He mentioned they had still not received the pathology slides .and they were critical to complete their diagnosis. We checked with Lansing and found out they had sent the wrong ones.

We had this corrected and they sent the right slides. We met with the doctor's nurse too and she said they would get those slides. No problem. They got lost again. Then a new nurse stepped in and we got all of our test reports. I really liked the new nurse, very efficient and from then on she was our contact with the proton doctor and reports didn't get lost. She also became our constant contact for appointments.

They informed us the proton treatments were very expensive but they were covered by our insurance. We were very glad to hear this as we had no idea of the cost but we knew it was in the thousands of dollars.

The Proton Center was an ultra modern facility that was

directly attached to the University of Florida Hospital and always had 20 or 30 patients waiting in large comfortable rooms near the treatment area.

Midge's Journal

MORE TUMORS—DEC. 15, 2009

From our motel at the Best Western ,we drove into the Florida Proton Institute in Jacksonville for more tests.

As of today I have had a PET scan that shows that I have NOT ONE but FOUR tumors in the right upper lobe of my lung. I met my proton doctor and I like him but not the new information he presented. It was not good. They found three new tumors.

It was not good. I think I went to stage four cancer. Ooooch.

Not a good day. I had to go to their old building for the PET scan and everything was rather old looking and seemed a bit disorganized to boot!! But I did get the test. Then they needed a blood work-up and I had to go about 8-9 miles to a private lab to get that done (not sure why for that one) and that was not a great place. The proton treatment area that we had all our hopes on, though was very ultra modern with a Star Wars look to it. We had to wait for our test results now and that would take awhile.

We went back to Bradenton for a few days and then came back. I met with the doctor and now they have to decide if my treatment should include surgery to remove that upper lobe mass. Then the proton/chemo regime might be a bit less? I have very mixed feelings at present on which I would prefer if it were up to me alone. The pain and risk in surgery is probably shorter (maybe) than with the chemo and radiation but of course I do not know that. My preference would be. Neither! Not a big fan of pain.

Jack's Journal

EXPLORING JACKSONVILLE

Until we know for sure Midge's treatment schedule, we decided to take a look at Jacksonville. Just drive around and see what is unusual in this city. The first thing we found is, it is easy to get lost, which we did.

This is also a city of bridge's all over the city and on the outskirts of the city. They are really beautiful and well designed, especially down town. Their shopping centers and stores were also fun to explore. Their art galleries were very well designed but needed more art and sculpture.

Chapter Six

Fourth Opinion

Midge's Journal

FOURTH OPINION—DEC. 18, 2009
A FIRM THERAPY SCHEDULE (PROTON & CHEMO)

They had me preparing for proton even before we had a firm schedule from all the doctors. The team of all the proton and chemo doctors are meeting tomorrow morning and then they will decide their specific course of action for my therapy.

After their meeting in the morning, Dr. Hoppe, my proton specialist, informed me that my treatment for proton would be five days a week for eight weeks (37 treatments) with chemo one day a week every Tuesday for eight weeks. Now at least I am in a firm program for treating my cancer. Of course once they do put it into remission, then how long will it stay that way? But for now I am thankful that I am in a program that has proven successful.. I do feel a lot better and very positive. ... for now.

SURGERY? MAYBE LATER

After twenty proton treatments and five chemo treatments they would decide if surgery was a good option as an alternative. At this point I am very positive.. But, I had no idea how tough chemo was going to get.

Midge's Journal

THE PROTON/CHEMO SURGERY TEAM—DEC. 19

Dr. Hoppe explained that I would have three docter's always monitoring my cancer treatments. Dr. Hoppe for proton therapy, an Oncologist for chemo and a another doctor for Surgery, . if that was needed at some point to remove the mass in my lung.

I got to get dressed and go to work-out a bit before breakfast. Have to see the chemo doctor this morning and then look for another place to stay on an extended basis that is nice, convenient, and does not cost a fortune..

CHEMO DOCTOR

I met with the Oncologist at the Baptist Hospital in Jacksonville. We found out he is one of the leading Oncologists in Florida. He was very kind and went over everything that happens during my chemo. I like him and my chemo treatments are here about a twenty minute drive from our condo. It is just past downtown.

Midge's Journal

THE PROTON TREATMENT
PREPARING FOR PROTON—DEC. 20, 2009

Yesterday I had a pulmonary test (not sure how I did) and then they got me all prepped for the proton by doing a simulation procedure. They had me lay on a PET scan table while they fitted me to a …looked like an air mattress material to start that they kept adjusting and adjusting to fit my body. I had to lay with my arms stretched tight overhead (and it really hurt before I was finished). They then took scans using chemical IV and more without.

Following that they marked my body with a bunch of very large "X"s all down both sides of my torso and down the front of my chest. This is to zero in on a spot during proton treatment. It was a bit unsettling to see my body afterwards and I have to leave this on all during the proton therapy.

Midge's Journal

NEED TO GET POSITIVE—DEC. 21, 7 AM

Woke very early this morning and so that is why I am writing here again. I have settled into the fact that I have cancer…that I will get a good kind of treatment to try to fight it off…and that until I start feeling bad or have more symptoms I am doing much better.. Once I start any of the former though…look out! I will not do good with that, especially the pain.

Midge's Journal

A PLACE NEAR THE PROTON CENTER—DEC. 22

Now that we had a firm schedule we started talking to friends at the Proton Center for ideas on where to stay. A number of places were suggested. One, an old mansion near the city park. We looked and expected to see some soldiers from the civil war as tenants (just kidding) it was kind of a gloomy, old place to visit with large chandeliers and high ceilings.

We finally found third and Main. A condo complex that is totally enclosed about a half a block square. It has good Security, with coded entry parking.. It has a kitchen and dining area with a separate bedroom and bath...no frills, bare walls but a handy location…only ten minutes from the Center. It also has a work-out room, elevator and a restaurant in the complex. It is primarily for patients of the Proton Center from the folks I have met. It seems ideal for us. Everyone we've met as we were looking at it seem very friendly and we will be working out with some of the other patients.

I should be able to keep in shape until the effects of the chemo start getting worse. Jack wants to start working out almost every day. He is also meeting some of the other patients that are here in this condo complex. A lot of them are prostate patients as that seems to be their specialty. Most of them are from the south but some are from the east coast area.

Midge's Journal

GOT OUR CONDO

We are now settled in and our lease starts on Jan. 1 and lasts as long as the treatments last or I last whichever comes first.

I have got to start thinking positive. . Jack really likes it here and wants me to plan on working out as soon as I can to keep in shape. It is in a very old section of the city that is being renovated.... a little scary at night.. It does have good security though.

OUR NEW CONDO—DEC. 23

We are getting use to our new place A nice one bedroom condo that is handy to the Proton Center.. There are 24 units here and it is pretty compact with a handy kitchen and all the utensils I think we need.

We spent the first couple weeks out by the airport in a Best Western and it was OK for the time. We have a GPS but traffic is crazy. The area where the Proton Center is located is not a great area either, so you want to know where you are going. From the papers it is the old section of the city. I still feel like we have good security though. The restaurant is handy and very busy on weekends. Usually we eat in and Jack buys groceries that are easy to fix. He is doing the fixing. I still feel fairly decent but weak. I am helping him fix some things that are easy to digest like asparagus soup. He cuts it up and adds milk and some spices for flavor. He seems to enjoy doing it.

Our rental is $1,500 per month which is not bad due to the location and the extras that I really do need because I will not be able to get around easy after awhile. I am a pretty sure of that from what I hear.

Midge's Journal

CHRISTMAS IN BRADENTON—DEC. 24-25

We went back to Bradenton just for Christmas between treatments and we spent a few days with Terry and Judy and Jack's nephew and wife who are also Terry and Judy Wallin. They stayed at our condo to spend Christmas with us. It was a nice Christmas and fun to have company. It was a nice break before all the chemo treatments. I also had a chance to talk to Peggy, John and Morgan, Steve and Don. Christmas was always a big event at our home on the Looking Glass River and this seems so far removed from that. Terry gave us a Christmas tree so I set that up and decorated it in our Condo. Then we spent Christmas day at Judy and Terry's where Terry cooked the Turkey…complete with pumpkin pie for dessert. I had sent gifts to all our kids and Judy had some kind of gift for everyone at the party which was fun. It was a nice Christmas but not like back home with all of our kids there at our home on the Looking Glass River. I always had the house all decorated for Christmas and the gifts under the tree flowed out all over the place. Steve, Don, Peggy, and John were always there with their spouses and also the grand kids. It was a joyful time with the large table in the dining room overflowing with food and pies. Jack always sat at the head of the table near the pies.

NEW YEARS EVE—A FUN SURPRISE PARTY

We are back in Jacksonville and met some friends taking treatments at the Proton Center. They invited us out to their RV park to celebrate New Year's eve with them and some others that are also from the Proton center and were having treatments there.

Terry and Judy came up for New Year's and we had a nice dinner and they went with us out to the RV park for cards and a little celebration. It was at a trailer park north of town. They were all fun people and I made some meatballs to share and everyone brought food and drinks. We sat around the tables and told jokes and told stories about other New Years Eve parties. I felt this was one of the nicest New Years Parties I had been to in a long time. Everyone was up and feeling good and even dancing at times. It was just a great time for a party and we all enjoyed it.. Some of them are leaving soon when their treatments are over.

We were all having a good time for a couple of hours…that is until I got sick and so did Jack (with a cold) and spent the next several days in misery. Nausea just would not go away. Finally got over it and found I needed to eat a little bit, but often, to keep something in my stomach. That seems to help along with the meds Terry and Judy left on Saturday and went back to their home in Bradenton, Florida.

Chapter Seven

Proton & Chemo

> The power of your love
> is so much stronger
> than my own
> I know I'll lose
> the battle
> if you call this
> loved one home
>
> I know only our prayers
> can change this
> rising tide
> so I pray
> you let me keep her
> for awhile…by my side
>
> — Jack Forsberg

Jack's Journal

PROTON AND CHEMO TREATMENTS—JAN. 1, 2010

The New Year started out poor. The very next day I got a bad head and chest cold and Midge was very sick from her chemo treatments. My brother and Judy were visiting and had to leave early because we were both in such bad shape. My cold actually continued for seven days and all that time I was really afraid Midge was going to get it. I can't think of anything worse than a chest cold with lung cancer. I prayed every day that Midge would not get it. We had enough on our plate as it was. I began sleeping on the couch to protect Midge from my cold. I finally got over the cold but by that time Midge was so sick I stayed sleeping on the couch. She was thrashing around and having a terrible time trying to sleep, and waking up all hours of the night. It was getting worse for Midge and the only thing I could think of was some kind of sleeping pills that wouldn't make her even sicker. Some of her meds do that to her. Tomorrow I will check with her doctor.

Jack's Journal

THE TREATMENT ROUTINE

It's Monday. I got ready and I took Midge to her proton treatment which usually lasts about an hour or so. Then Tuesday I took her to the chemo treatment which lasts five and a half hours. During this time I am spending most of my time in waiting rooms during her treatments. It is a sad place for a lot of relatives.

The chemo room is usually nearly full with other patients… sometimes I talk to them and it seems they want to tell me what their wife or husband or mother is going through at this time. It is almost always sad to hear and mostly due to heavy smoking. Thank God we are trying to stop it now. Too many people still don't believe it hurts them. They should just visit this place for awhile. I don't mind waiting because it has to be ten times worse on Midge and it is the least I can do is to be here if she needs me right after each treatment. Sometimes she is pretty down.

She doesn't feel well enough to go out so I buy all the groceries. I usually pick stuff easy to fix and what they say is good for Midge. It's a lot of soups and food that is easy to digest because her stomach is upset a lot of the time. She is losing some of her hair now and I know she feels terrible about that. I bought some hats but no, she wants to pick out her own naturally. She doesn't want a wig.

Jack's Journal

NEWSPAPER HEADLINE "RAPE IN OLD TOWN"

I picked up a newspaper and the headlines read "Rape Now Tolerated in Jacksonville?" A woman went into a bar and her car wouldn't start so she asked a guy she had been talking to if he would run her home. He did but on the way he stopped in a park and raped her. She went to the hospital and police but nothing happened. They said it was a bar in the old, rough part of town.

Midge asked where the bar was and I pointed out the window and said, "right down there about a block away from our condo. She said, wow, we won't go there.

We knew this was a rough part of town. The stores all have iron bars on all their windows and you can hear loud noises and guard dogs at night. Mostly, it's the guard dogs barking that keeps us up. So far, we haven't had a problem though, it is very secure. We feel pretty safe here.

Midge's Journal

JANUARY 6

I am in my third week of chemo and there have been many ups and downs. I had chemo yesterday and I feel like shxx today but nothing in particular. Not real nauseated like last week where I had it the whole time…just feel awful…not any one thing just overall.

I have to leave to have proton in a few minutes and maybe learn how I am doing with all of this. It won't surprise me if it's not good, from the way I feel. We are about five minutes from the proton center so that is good. I am supposed to let them know if I feel terrible but I haven't done that. I don't want to call if I can help it. My hair feels like cotton and I am losing long strands here and there but nothing major yet. I am expecting it to happen any day though. I need to get some sort of hat I like until I can go shopping for myself. We'll see...I feel lousy.

Midge's Journal

THE WORST WEEK OF MY LIFE—JAN. 9, 2010

It's been a real bitch of a week. Nausea never seems to really stop but not bad enough to up-chuck....just enough to make me feel really awful all the time. I want to sleep so much and I think it is because I hate the way I feel when I am awake. Nothing tastes good and water just turns my stomach but I have to drink lots of it. Starting to get me down that is for sure. I think I need to work on being up-beat but can't seem to muster the will to do it. My hair is now coming out. I just want to get this over with...and if it is not working I need to re-think all this stuff. I do really hope IT IS working, especially now.

Psyched up to the fact that we might get this cancer in check but I didn't like what I heard last week. I heard that it might get worse. I am not in a very good frame of mind right now. My hair comes out in handfuls. It really can't get much worse...or can it?

Jack's Journal

SAME DAY

Its been a terrible week for Midge. I am picking out groceries that I hope will help cut down on the up-chucking but Midge is hardly eating. I sure as hell hope we are getting close to the end of these chemo treatments. Midge has held up pretty well considering the number of times she has been sick to her stomach or the coughing spells. The blueberry yogurt seems to be one thing that she still likes and she will eat chicken noodle soup once in a while. She has to drink a lot of water and even that at times upsets her stomach. It is getting harder to find some food that she doesn't have a problem with. I spend a lot of time checking out food labels in the supermarket.

Overview (by Jack)

SELECTING SPECIAL FOODS

Like most men caring for a woman or an elderly person that is handicapped it is difficult to decide what to fix and how to fix it. First with Midge, I had to prepare food that was easy to digest and that was good for her condition. Due to her sore throat and her constantly upset stomach, it had to be easy to swallow as well as digest. The food also had to help build up her energy level and provide the basics to keep her as healthy as possible. Plus, it had to be food Midge liked to eat.

MIDGE'S FOOD SELECTIONS

Of course by now you know Midge. This was not something I was doing alone. Midge had very strong ideas on what she would like to eat and why. Luckily she loved blueberry yogurt which was an excellent choice for her.. It was easy to digest and was known as good for cancer patients and it helped protect her skin from wrinkles. She had very few during this time. I also selected "Boost" energy drink, macaroni, carrots, bananas, strawberries, roast chicken, chicken noodle soup, Cheerios and raisin bran cereals, asparagus tips soup, (made from scratch) watermelon and cantelope (Midges favorite) had to be fresh and ripe. She also liked simple salads with Neumann's ranch dressing.

Breakfast was cereal with milk and toast or poached eggs over raisin toast with blueberry muffins. She nearly always wanted morning coffee or juice. Once in a while grilled trout and boiled potatoes with carrots or peas at night. She skipped coffee only when her stomach was really upset. She had to drink a lot of water all the time.

Jack's Journal

A BAD MORNING—JAN. 20, 2010

The weekends seem to be worse than the mid-weeks for Midge. Today is Saturday and she is very sick--suffering from coughing up blood, very feverish and getting weaker every day. It is so damn frustrating not being able to do anything that seems to help. All I can do is see if we can find some new medicine to off-set the side effects of chemo and the proton. I am convinced some of the sharp chest pain may be caused from the proton treatments in her lung. So much for no side effects. She is sick almost every day except her chemo day. Probably the pain drugs take care of that one day. I don't know what else it would be. We need to find some better drugs to knock out the pain because Midge tolerates pain much better than normal. She is the only person I know that can take a root canal without any anesthesia. Tomorrow I will talk to the doctor and see if there is some medicine she can use to stop the nausea.

JAN. 29, 2010

This morning I woke up hearing Midge's coughing. A rough hard cough that was coming from way down deep. It is a new cough. When I asked how she slept, she said, "OK, but I was coughing up blood last night" It is red blood so it must be in my throat." Later she was coughing and there was no blood… thank God. According to her nurse, she is supposed to let them know and call the doctor when she has these bad side effects from the chemo because there may be a medicine that could help. But right now, Midge doesn't want me to call. It is beginning to seem like every day is a new pain or discomfort that makes it hard for Midge to relax or to sleep.

Each medicine is a test and it seems to me some of the pain is caused from the medicine. It is hard to tell. Midge started coughing up blood again but still doesn't want me to call. I really wonder how bad this chemo can get…it makes Midge weaker everyday and destroys her immune system. It seems like every day it's a little worse.

She finally had a little to eat and went to sleep. She is sleeping much more of the time now, just to get away from the pain. Damn, this is getting tougher every day. She is still on her full schedule of treatments for both proton and chemo. They may have to slow this down if this pain continues.

Chapter Eight

Bad Day At Flat Rock

Jack's Journal

BAD DAY AT FLAT ROCK—JAN. 30, 2010

Midge woke up coughing and had a hard time finding something to eat that would stay down. It is raining hard and it is supposed to rain all day. Midge broke down and cried because there was nothing I could do to help her get comfortable. I broke down and cried because there was nothing I could do to help her. I couldn't relieve the pain or suffering. Most of our proton friends are gone. They have finished their treatments. We have not left the condo all day. We are alone with only the doctors and each other to talk to.

It is a bad day at Flat Rock. Midge has taken her pain pill and can't take another for four hours. It still doesn't stop the pain. She just grits her teeth with it. This afternoon I got Midge to go down to the workout room. She said no 4 or 5 times but finally decided to go. This is the first time she has worked out for quite awhile. She did better than expected…at least she was able to sleep better. Plus, when she has enough strength to do it… it helps her want to eat something. She doesn't have much of an appetite most of the time and that worries me all the time.

Jack's Journal

A DAY FOR PRAYERS SUNDAY—JAN. 31, 2010

I got up early to go to church at the 8:30 service. Midge said she wanted to sleep. St. Mark's Lutheran was only having an early service today, not its 11:00 service. I have been to this church a few times now and the people were nice. It is a small church and they also have money problems. There was an older woman beside me in church and after church she started telling me she was from the Cape Cod area and her father was a ship captain for hunting whales. She said they had a place there for processing the whales and it was a big business back then. They sold the whale oil for all the oil lamps along the east coast. She said that was before ground oil wells were discovered in Pennsylvania; they were one of the whale oil firms in that area. They lost their business to the oil well people like Rockefeller. She said she was 98 years old. She seemed quite spry for her age.

I got back at the condo at 10:30 and Midge has vomited up her breakfast and her morning pills. She was really miserable. God, how bad can it get? She was going to lie down for awhile. She finally talked me into going down and eat breakfast at our restaurant that is attached to our condo complex. I knew she just wanted to be alone in her misery. I went down and worked out for awhile and tried to relax…and then went down and ate a sandwich and went for a walk.

After that we stayed in all day. I made Midge a bowl of chicken noodle soup and she only ate a little of it.

SHE SAID, "THIS IS THE WORST DAY OF MY LIFE"

Finally at 6:00 tonight, she called her doctor and told him how raw her throat was, how she was coughing up blood and the pain was worse. I was really glad she called him. I had never been able to convince her to call him before, though she has his home phone number and he told her to call if it got real bad. I can't imagine how it could get worse than this. She set up an appointment to see him first thing in the morning. I am glad of that too. The doctor's need to see how damn tough this gets. They may think the pain pills work. The hell they do. None of them work that well against pain that seems to never quit. One good thing is our son John called and he is talking about spending a few days with us in about ten days. Midge is concerned she may not be well enough to even handle his visit as much as she wants to see him.

Jack's Journal

MONDAY—FEB. 2, 2010

I got up this morning, went in and worked out for 20 minutes. Midge was too tired. Midge finally ate some breakfast but then up-chucked it and was really sick for awhile. She was supposed to be over for her proton treatment but was too sick to go for awhile. She called the chemo center to see what they had for her upset stomach. They said they would get something. I took Midge in to her doctor.

Her doctor checked Midge out and said she had a severe throat infection and he canceled her Tuesday chemo at the Baptist Hospital. He gave us a prescription for some drugs for her throat and made an appointment with a throat doctor tomorrow at 11:00.

The doctor also gave her some pills for the nausea. The chemo place called and asked Midge to come right in and they could also give her drugs to help lower the effects of the nausea. It would take about two hours. I dropped Midge off at the chemo center and went to a local pharmacy to get her various prescriptions and other things that her doctor ordered.

Jack's Journal

A BAD EXAMPLE FOR BAGGING—FEB. 4, 2010

First I drove around and found a large grocery store for food that Midge could swallow and keep down. It was a huge Winn Dixie store. It also had a drug store.

I came out with a cart full of groceries in plastic bags and a photographer stopped me and wanted to take photos of me filling up my car with plastic bags of groceries. He said he was with the local Jacksonville newspaper and they were doing a campaign to get people to stop using plastic. The photographer's name was Jon and he was staff photographer for the Florida Times Union. Jon lives forty miles west of Jacksonville. He likes to listen to books as he drives back and forth. He sounded just like our son John. He said the photos of me would be in the paper tomorrow morning. Sure enough, the next morning, I was on the front page. The waitress in the restaurant noticed my photo on the cover and said, "Is that you?" I said, "Yeah, I'm a bad example for using plastic." The next day, I gave Jon my son's e-mail address. They sounded so much alike and they both liked taking photos. My son did both photography and video at our ad agency.

Jack's Journal

THE NAUSEA & PAIN PATCH—FEB. 6, 2010

I picked Midge up from the chemo center and we went back to the condo about 6:00. About 9:00, Midge finally ate a little.

I've got to get her patch in the morning at the drug store. They said it wouldn't be ready until about 8:30 tomorrow. They are about 10 minutes away.

Next morning Midge and I met the throat doctor at 11:00. I hope Midges throat clears up... They have changed her chemo to Thursday AM... The doctor said this patch was voted one of the top 10 best medical products of 2008. I just hope it works. It is supposed to help eliminate some of the sickness caused by continual chemo treatments. After she had used it awhile I couldn't see any change but Midge said it may have helped the nausea. It was expensive. We had a major problem with our insurance paying for it. I had to pay a good portion of it to get it.

Jack's Journal

THURSDAY TREATMENT—FEB. 8, 2010

This has been a fast week and now Midge is into her chemo treatment again. She actually did pretty well.

This morning before she went in. She is feeling better today. She had to be in treatment by 9:30 so I ran around and got some drugs for her. I had to go to two different drug stores and fought with the insurance company to get a refill on her medicine that helps prevent her having the dry heaves. The nurse pulled a few strings at the chemo dept. and one of the managers at the drug store finally came through and gave me her refill for nothing. He got a high five from me on that. We are fighting the insurance company almost every day on the cost of prescriptions. It is very obvious they feel the costs of all the bills are running too high. They still need better medicine for pain, it still doesn't stop it as Midge will testify.

CHEMO LOUNGE PATIENTS

As I was waiting in the chemo lounge I talked to a man that, from a distance, looked very healthy. He sat down next to me and we started talking. This is his history for the last few months.

In August he went in for triple bypass heart surgery. He had problems with it and ended up for three or four weeks in the hospital and a built in heart monitor. Then he found out he had throat cancer and they started him into a program that included 24 days of some chemo and radiation treatments. About three quarters way through these treatments he developed a large hole in his stomach and he had to have an emergency operation that nearly killed him. I had the feeling he had come from some other area of the country. He said his chemo treatments effected him the worst. Now he is very weak and can barely talk. He said he can't taste anything. His treatments are over. He didn't say where he was treated at and I didn't ask him. He is here to see if they can help him with his voice as he can barely talk. After he told me this he said he had to stop talking as it tired him out to talk. We shook hands and he went into one of the rooms. This is just one of the many stories I heard while waiting for Midge in the chemo lounge. I never tell Midge about these cases unless they are very positive. Many times the people in the waiting lounge were mostly the relatives of the patients in for their chemo treatments. I met many husbands or wives that were waiting the five and half hours it took for their spouses treatment. Once in a while I would go down to the drug store on the lowest level and get one of Midge's drugs. There was also a small café there that you could get a coffee or simple sandwich while your prescription was being filled. Everyone seemed to know you were waiting on a chemo patient upstairs. Most of them wanted to tell you their story about the effects of their spouses smoking habits. Almost always they mentioned how much their partner smoked, some even now, right after their treatment. You couldn't help but feel bad for them. Many gave the impression, 'It is their own fault.'

Chapter Nine

My Son's Visit

MY SON'S VISIT—FEB. 10, 2010

We just came back from Midge's proton treatment and we had good news. The proton doctor arranged to have her Friday proton treatment at 9:30 at night so John can actually see how the proton treatments are handled. After talking to patients this afternoon I am sure glad we got Midge into the proton treatment for her cancer therapy. At least her side effects from proton are not nearly as bad as the radiation treatments.

We got our dinners tonight from KFC. It is only a few blocks from us. Midge ate most of hers. We are both looking forward to seeing John tomorrow night. Midge took quite a few pills to keep her from getting sick so much, so hopefully she will feel better when John arrives tomorrow. I am sure the whole family will want to quiz John on how things are going with their mother. John will handle that very well. I also know Midge will act better than she feels.

We were both excited to see our son John and he seemed happy to see us. This had been a long haul through a lot of pain and frustration for his mother. She was quite concerned that she may not be well enough to handle the visit, but John finally arrived and we were both really glad to see him. Midge was sick, though, and John and I went down to breakfast by our selves to the restaurant next door. I can tell John is surprised at how sick his mother is. Actually I know Midge is trying very hard to act better than she really feels. We had a good talk and I explained to John how the treatments were going and how hard it was to find the right drugs to stop the nausea and the pain... more like impossible...but I didn't tell him that. I did tell him I think we are near the end of the treatments so I hope for some good news very soon if their forecast works...and I pray it does.

It was great seeing him and we went over all the details of the treatments so he could tell the others in our family what was happening to their mother...and hoping things would soon get better. I know John will handle it well with Peggy and Don and especially with Steve. I know Steve is going through his private hell worrying about his mother. Thank God he is not here to see it, as I am very sure that would be a lot worse for him and his mother.

Midge's Journal

PREP & PET SCAN—FEB. 13, 2010

It was an interesting week to say the least. We are in Jacksonville on Monday and I'm coming down with a head cold of all things. Have not felt up to par (my post-cancer treatment part is a bit hard to determine) for a couple weeks. I can only say .just in general...I don't feel good! I have no energy, and cough quite a bit, mostly in the morning.

I got a Pet Scan coming up. I don't know what they expect to find...something good I hope but right now I don't know. I haven't had much to eat this morning and I am not really hungry. I think this is one of the scans to see how the program is progressing, or not. We'll see. I know we should be close to the end.

Midge's Journal

FOUR HOURS... DON'T MOVE

Anyway, they got the PET Scan done Tuesday AM. and I managed to get through the 4 hours of prep and tests pretty good. Didn't cough or sneeze during the critical part. I had to stay perfectly still 21 minutes which is the longest period that you must stay very still with your arms extended tightly over your head till you think they will pop out of their sockets any time. I feel a little stiff all over and a little sore. I am really glad that it's over and now maybe I can get some rest. My arms are sore but it usually goes away pretty quickly.

I am going back to our condo and collapse and go to sleep for an hour or so. I am just tired all over right now. My bed is going to feel real good.

Midge's Journal

A FEW HOURS LATER

I went back to the condo and rested and asked Jack to go do a movie or something so he didn't have to just sit and watch me be miserable because I was getting worse (head cold) all the time. I talked Jack into going to see the King's Speech which he was a bit reluctant to do at first, but finally he went to see it.

When he came back he raved about it. It was up his WWII alley. He said that was a very decisive time in British history and that speech was the beginning of war with Germany. Also It was at a time when Hitler felt he had England backed against the wall and he was going to finish them off. That speech so aroused the people of England that it helped change the course of history. He said it was a great movie. Of course Jack had an

English roommate for about five years from London so Jack is steeped in the history of England. I have heard all about Churchill and all the generals over there. He and his roommate John Wade use to argue who was the best generals during the war. Like who cares, I just want to get over this cold. I still got the same cough. Can't seem to get rid of it.

Chapter Ten

Cancer Results Proton & Chemo

Midge's Journal

WAITING FOR FINAL RESULTS

So Wednesday morning we meet my doctor to find out how the cancer is doing. Because I have felt so poorly for the last few weeks I wouldn't have been surprised to hear something not so good even fatal…but I was hoping that wouldn't be the case of course. If miraculously this turns around, I still want to schedule our delayed trip to Rome. This was my dream before all this treatment started. It was a good idea that we both decided we would do. This was to be the beginning of our "Bucket List" before we were too old to enjoy it. We didn't expect this though, so it put a hammer on all our plans to say the least.

Midge's Journal

GOOD NEWS, CANCER IN REMISSION

Jack and I met with the doctor after they read the PET Scan and I am free of cancer. No signs at all. This cancer news could not have been better. NO new activity in my body. PERIOD (hmmmmm, they didn't do my brain this time though so?

Anyway, we were elated to hear that of course. I had worn a mask to protect my nurse and doctor and others from my 'head cold" but now a head cold don't seem bad at all.

Dr. Hoppe checked me over and listened to my lungs and looked in my throat, then said he was giving me a prescription for antibiotics just to be safe because of my lung issues.

CONGRATULATIONS, MIDGE, YOU MADE IT!

My voice still sounds scratchy the same way it has for months. Both Dr. Hoppe and his nurse congratulated me on finally putting the cancer into remission. They said there was some grey area on the scan but hopefully not anything to worry about. I could hug both Dr Hoppe and Keri for all the work they did to get me well... I will be forever thankful for both of them. It was a long haul but they were there when I needed them. I will still be going back to them for check- ups every six months or so.

Midge's Journal

I CAN HARDLY BELIEVE IT

We left the Proton Center feeling very upbeat, but I still wasn't feeling well...very weak and shaky. But now we were heading home and that was GREAT.

We packed and were ready to hit for our condo in Bradenton, Florida. I feel elated that I put the cancer into remission but why didn't I feel better. Probably the cold and the drugs, plus my throat infection. But we decided to go anyway.

But I was coughing and getting worse all the time. I up-chucked before we hit the I-75 interstate. What a mess, so we stopped and I cleaned up for the long trip to Bradenton. It would be a four to five hour trip. We stopped to eat in a little restaurant but all I could have was soup and then it didn't set too well. It was a long trip and I kept getting worse.

At 4:30 PM I called my lung doctor's office in Sarasota from my cell and she told me I'd better get to ER as fast as I could because I sounded awful. She wanted me in the ER in Sarasota Hospital where my lung doctor practiced from his office nearby. Jack was glad to hear I could get in fast with my doctor.

Midge's Journal

SARASOTA EMERGENCY ROOM

I am so short of breath and wheezing badly plus the cough. At first I didn't want to go to ER but Jack was firm that I should and I could see this was not going well so we went right on past Bradenton to Sarasota Memorial Hospital. Of course I know the routine well.. We will be in ER for hours after arriving. It was about 5:30 PM when we got admitted. Jack was really exhausted from having to do all the driving plus now waiting in the ER. Of course he fell asleep several times in ER but it was a long night. He went home when they told me I would be admitted which was about 11:00 PM. I finally was in my room at about 1 AM. The room was quite pleasant and had a window near the bed with a bath close by along with a vanity sink. I am now sacked in for the night. They said I will have respiratory treatments every four hours and tests on my vitals, plus pokes, IV's and the works. Nothing that new, just the regular list of tests I've had before.

Through the night my roommate who appears to be a very

ill young girl, guessing her age as in her twenties, coughs so loud and uncontrollable it would make me jump when she started. Of course I chimed in now and then but not to HER degree. I was afraid she had something worse that I might get too.

Midge's Journal

SARASOTA HOSPITAL ROOM NEXT DAY

At one point I wanted to go for a walk around the hallway so I could get some exercise after lunch and she was sitting up in bed with her eyes open and I made eye contact and said 'Hi, how are you doing?' She stared at me … Very cold. No comment. She apparently has a lot of problems with drugs or alcohol….. kidney failure, potassium, and so on. It's now Friday, the family was in by her bed along with her boy friend. They told her if she refused to do any of the tests they would have to discharge her. She did agree to a CT scan of her gall bladder. I don't know what happened there as to the results.

Midge's Journal

STILL A BAD COUGH

In the meantime here I am not progressing like I hoped and I am sure these people hoped I would too. Still awful cough but even with every four hour breathing treatments, I am wheezing so loud they can hear me in the hall as they enter the room. Plus I am so short of breath it gets a bit scary. Was told there is something else going on with my lungs other than the effects of cancer. That's nice. The cancer doesn't do me in, but whatever the hell this is sure could and a couple times I wondered how this was really going to shake down. After visiting hours on Saturday I had 'messed' with my computer a lot but decided to try to sleep about 8:30 PM.

STRANGE HAPPENINGS

Then things started to get a bit strange behind the curtain. Someone was peeking around it to look in my direction. I guess to see if I was asleep. With my terrible breathing they probably were sure it was a 'snore' from some Old Broad. Well pretty soon the tall, long pony tailed, very scruffy boyfriend went by my bed to use the bathroom. They are supposed to be for just patients but Jack and other visitors use them so....no problem. BUT, he is in there a very long time. Flushes once but does not come out. Long time again so I look at the clock and after another 5 minutes or so another flush and he comes out and quickly went by my bed. My eyes are "almost" closed and with no light on it would appear as if they were, I supposed and hoped.

Now the activity behind the curtain really gets going. It is a "sorry baby", "yeah, I know baby" the rest was undetectable by my old ears anyway. All the time this head is now and then peeking around the curtain at me. I am a bit nervous by now. Then the tall pony tail boy friend goes to the bathroom one more time, and this time passing my bed I see him put "something" in the needle disposal canister that hangs on the wall at the foot of my bed. He didn't even hesitate, hits it right on. Yeah, I know what you're thinking, so was I. Well, I am getting out of this funk. I need to get past this kind of downer and FAST.

Chapter Eleven

Bedside Mystery Over

Midge's Journal

'SIDE FRUSTRATION' — 8:45 PM

Right here close, I have a vanity mirror and sink…all right beside the window. A patient's bed is so close it is a bit uncomfortable to brush your teeth, do your hair or any such personal things with her laying 4 feet away trying hard not to look at me. So today the lady has dialysis and I am going to get a shower and do my hair finally! She left about 5 PM and will be gone approximately four hours. They prepared the shower for me (special mats and towels etc) and say okay. She leaves and I am going to finally be able to clean up and maybe, just maybe, do a few things that have been alluding me to boot. Privacy and time.

Yippee. I get undressed ready to shower and…..Oh No, I need a plastic bag to cover my IV and not get it wet. No problem…and 5:20 I call down to the desk and they say it will be a couple minutes.

It is now 5:59 PM and I am still sitting here. I tried to find something to make some cover for myself but no luck so do I call again? Do I wait? Do I just give up and forget the shower. My frustration is mounting even though I have time. However, she has lots of relatives that come in all the time and I know there will be some waiting for her return, so need to get this done and besides…..I am on STEROIDS and I want it NOW.!

Oops… Here comes a cleaning girl down the hall. I asked if she had a plastic bag an walla…I have a plastic bag and with rubber band from my check book I am off to the shower and should have shower, hair done, lotions applied, teeth brushed, a bit of make up may help. I don't know why except I always feel better if I LOOK better. I should even get this all done before 7 pm and I did! FANTASTIC. Finally a plan works out. So now when Jack gets here, I feel like a human being again… all spruced up and ready to go. I sure feel better. I should be out of here today unless they find something else. I am going to be sleeping in my own bed back in our condo. GREAT!

Jack's Journal

LIFE IN OUR CONDO IN BRADENTON—APRIL 10, 2010

It has been a long time since I have written on what has happened to Midge over the last six weeks here in our condo in Bradenton, Florida. For Midge it has been a roller coaster of pain, hope and sleeping nightmares. The sleep was to avoid the pain. For the first few weeks here there were the massive coughing spells that were mostly false heaves. They were very painful and left her throat raw. The doctors tried a series of drugs with almost no positive effects. This went on for over a month. The doctors are trying different drugs. They still think it may be the high pollen count in Florida.

MANATEE MEMORIAL HOSPITAL

Finally I got Midge back in the Manatee Hospital to find what is causing the rough cough and the back pains. Midge ended up in the emergency ward of Manatee hospital late at night and they ran a mass of tests and still did not cure it. They did slow it down some but that is all. We were sure it was a direct result of the cancer treatments but found out later it was probably activated by the high pollen count in Florida. We are now in a frantic quest to find out what is this weird thing that is causing Midge so much pain every day. We have not heard any one thing that makes sense and it has been going on now for weeks.

Jack's Journal

SEVERE BACK PAINS APRIL 15, 2010

Midge started with pains in her lower back which over a few weeks become increasingly worse and more painful. Finally it was stabbing pains that could not be calmed even with heavy doses of morphine. No matter how she sat, laid or moved. In the middle of the night we went to emergency at Manatee Hospital. They ran all the usual tests, blood, urine, X-rays of the chest checking the body for muscle pain, etc.

Jack's Journal

FIRST OPINION, MUSCLE SPASMS

The doctor's concluded it was muscle pains with spasms. They gave her pain medicine and muscle relaxers. The pains continued and by the following week were back in full force… screaming pains. On a scale of 1 to 10, they were up to 12. Beyond Midge's ability to stand it and she did root canals with no pain killers We desperately needed a cure for Midge's excruciating pain.

SECOND OPINION, GALL STONES? ANOTHER NEW DOCTOR

At six in morning the following week we went to the emergency room at Manatee Memorial Hospital in Bradenton. The doctors ran tests and more tests and finally found the answer. They were convinced the cause of the pain was stones in the gall bladder. At last they felt they had found the true cause for the pain. Now at least they can cure Midge and stop the pain. At least that is what the doctor is saying.

Early the next day a gall bladder surgeon removed Midges gall bladder. The surgery went well and the pain was not as sharp as it had been, but you expect pain from an operation… even with limited invasion surgery. We were on the verge of finally being content that this pain would now go away and we could start enjoying life again. Midge had to stay an extra day in the hospital to receive two large bladder bags of blood due to the operation. It took all day to transfer the blood. She was very quiet and very down.

A FEW DAYS LATER…THE TERRIBLE PAIN RETURNS

I took Midge home but the pain did not go away. It got progressively worse each day. Finally it was so bad we were back in the emergency ward at Manatee Memorial with tests and more tests. The doctor that did the gall bladder operation came in and assured Midge he would find the cause and cure it. Four hours later I called that doctor and he said they had found the pain was not caused by the gall bladder and therefore there was nothing more he could do with it.

He suggested we go to an internal medicine specialist. We began to question the need for the gall bladder operation. What is causing this severe pain that so damn painful for

Midge? Obviously the doctors don't know and don't seem to have a clue. Both of us at this time are beginning to question our doctors. They just seem to be putting the answer on pollen or whatever else pops up. There is no firm conclusion as to what is actually causing this severe pain for Midge.

Jack's Journal

THIRD OPINION: HAS THE CANCER RETURNED?

One of the tests for cancer was an MRI which provides very specific details of the body area. We were already to question our doctors at this point.

The nurse suggested her doctor, a new doctor on staff that agreed to look at midge's tests. So we called him and he agreed to look at the tests and order more tests. Early the next morning he was at Midge's bedside even before I got there and said they had found a mass that was on the spinal column and he would have it tested but it could be a new cancer. If it was cancer this may be only the one place it has appeared.

Both of us broke down and cried at this point. I called this doctor and he told me the same thing he had told Midge earlier in the morning. This was devastating news….about the worst news we could receive after all the hell that Midge had already survived fighting the cancer into remission.

I called Dr. Hoppe in Jacksonville and talked to him about it and he said it was very possible but he needed all the tests to confirm it. He said I will get back to you as soon a I have studied the test results.

Chapter Twelve

Finding A Miracle

Jack's Journal

MORNING

I called John and eventually we talked to Steve and Peggy and Don. Peggy said later she cried for over three hours on her drive to Traverse City. We thought this was the final blow. We were both crying and we had no idea what to do next. I said let's wait until Dr. Hoppe has confirmed it to be sure it has spread. We were both talking to the kids and crying and trying to think of anything that could be done but this looked like the straw that broke the camels back. It was the worst news we could possibly get. We were both sure this was not the end of her pain nightmare and the cancer was back…maybe now on her spine.

A FEW HOURS LATER

I am sure both Midge and I had hit bottom at this point. Through all the trials and proton and chemo and tests… there was always hope. This incident seem to be the end of it all. Midge was sobbing and so was I. It was like the gates were open and we both just let it ALL spill out. We had tried everything and lost…that is the way it felt. We had relayed this same feeling to our kids and that was equally painful. We knew we left them sobbing for their mother. Midge. was at the lowest point in her life and so was I.

MIDGE'S GUARDIAN ANGEL PRAYS FOR A MIRACLE

About two hours into this heart breaking scene, a man walked in and introduced himself as Ray Nelson a Non Denominational Chaplain. We explained what had just happened. And he seemed very deeply concerned. He said you may not believe it but I have seen many 'miracle cures" but Midge said she did want to pray for a miracle, but for strength to handle what had just happened to her.

We all got down on our knees and held hands around Midge's bed. He asked God's power to remove this burden from Midge. It was a very powerful prayer and we were all crying all the time he was praying.

When it was over both Midge and I felt like a weight had been lifted off our shoulders. Even if the facts were the same, we felt much better. The Chaplain left us alone. After the prayer I went out in the lobby and met Mr. Nelson and thanked him for his help. I told him about a book I had just read, *There are No Atheist in Foxholes*, He said he was in Desert Storm and met some Israeli soldiers and they told him this story. They had several tanks in a column in the desert and a mine explosion blew up one of their vehicles. They discovered they had wandered into a large minefield with no way out except through it. They knew no matter which way they went someone was going to get killed. They all got together and prayed.

Right after the prayer a tornado like wind came up and wiped the desert clean around them… exposing all the mines so they could be easily dismantled They removed the mines with no problem. They had never had a roaring strong wind start and stop like that before. They thanked God.

THE FOURTH OPINION—NEW DOCTOR
5:00 PM SAME DAY, APRIL 25, 2010

About five that afternoon a doctor we had never seen before walked into Midge's room…a Dr. Phil Plousy.

He said he had looked over Midge's tests and he had found another reason for her pain. He said he was a Radiation Oncologist and at many times his patients would experience this pain after extensive radiology. He explained how this could happen. He said he had no idea what the spot on the spine was…it could be something that had always been there. He said there is a thin layer of material between the lung inner surface and the lung outer wall and when it is flexible there is no problem, but when it becomes hard due to radiology, it becomes stiff and this causes extreme pain. If it is treated with steroids it goes away over time. I saw your chart and I felt this could be the cause of your pain. I had them put in a very small amount of steroid into your drip container. I hope that may help relieve some of your pain.

The nurse brought in Midge's pain pills.

Suddenly we all realized Midge had been "pain free" for several hours. Even more remarkable, Midge's pain was gone for good. The nuclear bone scan test came back and showed no signs of cancer. We were absolutely dumbfounded. We thanked God.

During this time we received a call from Dr. Hoppe saying they found no indication of cancer. This was the second time that Dr. Hoppe had corrected another doctors diagnosis of possible cancer in Midge.. If you do not work daily with proton he said, you cannot recognize the after effects of the proton as we found out several times..

We never saw Mr. Nelson again so he has no idea what happened. I am sure he was one of God's chosen helpers for people in horrible pain. I believe that if you truly believe in miracles, God will respond to your prayers.

Midge and I belong to a small Lutheran church in Tustin, Michigan with a congregation of only 30 or 40 parishioners. From cards and letters I feel very sure almost every one of them was praying for Midge's recovery. **I also believe God listens.**

Jack's Journal

SATURDAY—APRIL 27, 2010

What a miraculous recovery. We are almost beside ourselves with joy even though it is raining outside this morning, the sun is shining on the inside. What a relief it is. We are out of Manatee Hospital and back in our condo for a few days of rest and relaxation.

Midge had a good night's sleep last night and went shopping with Judy and Cil today with no pain. She ate a big breakfast about three in the afternoon at Denny's. I picked her up at Judy and Terry's right after my golf game. She bought a new watch at the Red Barn. Her old one had stopped in the hospital. She noticed it the day we left the hospital. I said maybe now your new life begins.

Midge's Journal

BRADENTON, FLORIDA, SUNDAY—APRIL 28, 2010

We are going to church today on Anna Marie Isle near Bradenton with friends from Tustin. I am almost afraid to say things have turned around as they are so much better. I am afraid I might be wrong again. I now have six hats color coded to all my summer outfits. They feel and look great, and I am sure my hair will return. The roller coaster ride is over for now. It is still raining outside but who cares, it's beautiful. We are looking forward to going back up north to Tustin, Michigan and see all our old friends. I have a stack of cards from friends a foot high…all saying they are praying for me. There is no doubt in my mind. **The Lord Listens.**

Midge's Restoration

The smile is back on Midge's face
the laugh back in her voice
all I can say is "thank you Lord"
at last we can rejoice

We are beyond
that painful mountain
past months of stress and strain
because a strange thing happened
that's just hard to explain
from deep despair
a Chaplain's prayer
set her free from pain

I feel like a prisoner
that's now served his time,
walking in the sunshine
absolved of all my crimes

No longer will I hold my breath
from the fear that cancer brings
I'll join the world and dance
and Midge and I will sing
And I know I could fly
if only I had wings

—Jack Forsberg, April 2 010

Chapter Thirteen

Midge's "Bucket List"

Jack's Journal

HOME AGAIN—MAY, 2010

After the final medical OK in Jacksonville we went back to our log home near Tustin, Michigan and started finalizing the plans for Midge's **"Bucket List".** We were beside ourselves with joy. Midge had defeated cancer and was in full remission…no other side effects. We were ecstatic. Our first trip would be to Yellowstone Park, a place Midge had always wanted to visit and now we were going and we felt great. We also enjoyed seeing and spending time with all our Tustin friends that had been so supportive throughout all the cancer treatments. The Augustana Lutheran Church in Tustin became our favorite place to meet and enjoy our old friends.

MIDGE'S "BUCKET LIST" —YELLOWSTONE NATIONAL PARK

Midge and I planned a bucket list that included all of the places she wanted to visit. We started with Yellowstone National Park. We went with Terry, my brother, and his wife Judy. Terry drove and we got there too late to take the tour bus, so we paid a guide and driver and she took us all over the park. We saw all kinds of buffalo, elk, bear and other game as well as all the waterfalls, geysers and a great boat ride on the beautiful lake.

Our guide also took us to see Old Faithful where it was spewing up steam 40 or 50 feet into the air. It is a scene we both wanted to see and enjoy and to share it on this special trip. The next stop was another of the trips we always wanted to make and never did.

MONUMENT VALLEY—THE PRESIDENTS SCULPTURE

The next place we all wanted to see was where the Presidents are carved in stone on the top of a very large mountain. It is a WOW!. at first glance. How any one man could accomplish this is simply almost unbelievable. We went through all the rooms and read all about the sculptor and his work of making it all fit closely together without destroying any part of it. We also went to the giant Indian head on top of the mountain. It is a work in progress but what a gigantic piece of sculpture. I had read a lot about the Indian culture and it was a very special place for any Indian..no matter what tribe. They would have a monument that would last forever..

THE BLACK HILLS—WILD BILL HICKOCK'S DEMISE

Then all of us went to the Black Hills and golfed up in the mountains. We golfed with some guys from the local casino and got free dinners from them for all of us at the casino. Midge and Judy spent time in the local casinos while us guys golfed on the side of the local mountain… the highest golf course I have ever played on. Very exciting. When Terry and Judy came down for breakfast I had winners on three Lucky Seven machines….a few hundred dollars. Midge was lucky too on her video poker machines. Midge had always been very lucky at cards and poker and she proved again that she had a special talent.

DEADWOOD SOUTH DAKOTA

We also stopped in a bar where Wild Bill Hickock was shot in the back. They re-enacted that scene for us and a large group of Chinese. It was a typical wild west town of the Old West., The shooting was in the same bar and same seat where Wild Bill was delt his aces and eights for the last time.

FALL COLOR TOUR IN THE UP

In the fall we continued to take color tours of Michigan's Upper Peninsula and Wisconsin. We would take The Badger ship from Ludington and sail over to a port near Green Bay, and then drive north through the woods. We would also stop along the coast in Munising at Pictured Rocks then on into Sault St Marie, Michigan. We went across the entire state from the farthest point west back to Sault St. Marie. It was a beautiful trip with the fall colors at their brightest.

We played golf at the Wild Bluff Golf Course and the women played at the casino in Brimley .next door. Vic and Cil Eastlund joined us on our UP colored tours with Terry, Judy, Midge and me. We always had a lot of fun and couldn't wait to go back..The view from the top of Wild Bluff allows one to see Lake Superior and in the morning with the misty clouds climbing up from below there is a panoramic lake scene that will take your breath away. Golfers feel like they are hitting the ball into a layer of clouds below. It's a new experience. The color's of the woods in the fall are always breathtaking and this year it was especially so in both Wisconsin and Michigan.

LONDON, ENGLAND TO ST. PETERSBURG, RUSSIA

We flew from Detroit, Michigan to London, England. We toured London for a few days with a rented guide. We hit all the famous tourist spots as well as traveling on the underground. I got separated from Midge, Terry, and Judy and got lost on the shady side of London. I had a few scary experiences finding my way back to our hotel. Later we took a bus to the white cliffs of Dover on our way to our Holland of America cruise ship We visited Estonia, Germany then on to St. Petersburg, Russia. We visited their large art galleries where they had the Mona Lisa and a host of other famous paintings and sculpture. We were treated to a vodka tasting ceremony in one of the hotels that left us all a little wobbly. They have some beautiful churches with those elaborate domes. Then we stopped and spent time in Sweden, Finland and Denmark and flew to Amsterdam, Holland before we flew back to Detroit, Michigan and then home to Tustin, Michigan. We all had a great time on the trip, collecting a lot of great photos and memories. Midge loved the street music in Sweden.

ROME AND THE VATICAN

Our next trip was a favorite of Midge's. We went first to Rome. This was just Midge and I, where she located a nice hotel about two blocks from the Vatican. We stayed there for a week as part of a cruise around France, Sicily, North Africa and Italy; a really great tour. We were in the Vatican on Sunday. We were allowed to have High Mass in the holy area of the large cathedral with all the priests, and a very large male choir present for their main communion of the week. The area where the Pope has communion and we went to where Michelangelo spent so much time working on the ceiling. It is hard to see because it is so high, but we also loved his sculptures such as the Pieta of Christ and Mary.

We also visited all the major historical sites in Rome including the Parthenon which was one of my favorites. It is so high and with that large hole in the ceiling. It never rained on us inside although it was raining while we were there. It is the place where Raphael the painter is buried and you can see his casket. We both liked the sculptured waterfalls throughout Rome as well as General Hadrian's buildings all over the Italian countryside as well as North Africa. We took a bus tour outside of Rome to Hadrians huge estate in the high hills of Italy. It was full of sculptures and specially designed areas with large water landscapes surrounded with rooms and artifacts. He was one of the very best leaders of Rome colonizing the countries he conquered into the ways of the Roman people. He treated the people with respect especially those from Greece. We also spent one great day in Southern France on the beaches admiring the bathing beauties and had a fabulous lunch that was also quite unusual with the special wines and all the trimmings.

ALASKA AND VANCOUVER, CANADA

Another area Midge really enjoyed was Alaska. We flew to Anchorage and explored that area and then went by bus to Seward where we joined Holland America's cruise to the cities of Haines, Juneau, Skagway and Ketchikan… Every town there was unusual and full of unique spots to visit. Midge loved the Indians delicately carved totem poles. We could watch them carving for days on one design. We took a special boat to see the whales and glaciers as well as the seals on an island of their own. It was exciting stuff with good weather, not cold at all. We enjoyed great food and lots of fish and seafood dishes of every kind. Alaska has so many places to visit and is so much fun. The huge glaciers were so beautiful and they seem to be moving all the time. Huge ice cliffs were slopping into the water with a massive crashing sound always before I could get my camera ready to shoot. We went down the ocean to Vancouver, Canada, and stayed in a nice hotel there and next day explored the city. We met some friends from Florida and toured the city and parks that were so well designed with all kinds of waterways and sculptured parks all along the huge bay area. The next day we flew back to Grand Rapids, Michigan. We met our son and his wife and then drove to our home on the Pine River with lots of photos and memories.

MIDGE'S CONTACT WITH THE PROTON CENTER

Midge set up an agreement with the Proton Center that she would stop by every six months and have a CT scan done to check for cancer. The intervals coincided with our trips to Florida and back to Michigan every six months. Each time for four and half years the results were always the same. No Cancer.

On two different occasions other doctor's had found evidence they felt was the spread of a new cancer. In each of these cases, the Proton Center reviewed all the evidence and sent back a clean bill of health for Midge. Each time was quite emotional as you can imagine Also during this span of time that Midge was cancer free we sold our home on the Looking Glass River north of Grand Ledge, Michigan and moved to our log home on the banks of the Pine River just west of Tustin,,

Michigan. During this time Midge and I visited our friends in Tustin and also enjoyed our condo on the golf course in Brfadenton, Florida.

Jack's Journal

EDITING AND PUBLISHING

During this cancer free time we stayed at our log home on the Pine River. I wrote three books and Midge edited and published them all. She also did a lot of work on the cover and design of the books. The books titles are listed in the back of this book.

Midge also edited and published a very special lifetime poetry book for my brother Terry. It took her about two months to do his book alone. She never charged him a dime for it and she said it was remarkable that he was able to do so many poems over the years. He sent many books to his friends and they were equally impressed at the quality of his poems.

Over four years after she had put the cancer into remission we were back down to our condo in Bradenton, Florida. During the first of December of 2013 Midge started having coughing problems and her throat was very raw. We soon found out this was the beginning a series of problems that would not get that much better over the next few months.

Jack's Journal

MIDGE'S NEW LUNG DISEASE—DEC. 2013

After over four years the side effects from the cancer in Midge's already damaged lung left her with a weak immune system that made her vulnerable to other diseases. such as a rare lung disease with no known cures. In December 2013 it started to take its toll on Midges health. After many hospital visits and a final stay in Blake Hospital in Bradenton, Florida Midge wanted to go home to our log home on the Pine.

She had endured five months of heavy medical treatments to try and stop a rare virus identified by Atlanta's research staff as an incurable disease. It left her heart and lungs so weak she was struggling to breathe. We made plans with a special medical plane to fly her home. My brother Terry paid for this specially equipped plane and crew which was very expensive. She was flown by this medical plane crew to Grand Rapids, Michigan where she stayed a few days and then on to our log home on the Pine River near Tustin, Michigan. It was .almost exactly five years since the cancer was put into remission at the new proton center in Florida.

She had a very special Mothers Day with all the family. She was tired but she bravely pretended to be much better than she felt. She was smiling and talking very personal to each member of the family. Steve had come home from Las Vegas and Don from Colorado. Peggy, Dan, Lindsay and little Emma and Colon were also there to say good by to their beloved mother and gramma. I was so glad we had made it back to our log home It was what we were both praying for the last few weeks. At last, we had made it in time. Peggy, Steve, Don and John also had time to talk to Midge in private and say their goodbyes.

Toward evening Midge seemed to get a rush of spirit and was more animated with her smiles and she looked happy. Midge smiled and said "Goodbye? Where do you think I am going?" She passed away that evening. She just went to sleep with a nice look on her face like she was very content.

Midge's Funeral

Midge had a beautiful funeral with two ministers…both friends of hers in the Lutheran church in Tustin, Michigan with all of her friends present. I am sure the Lord welcomed Midge home with open arms. From the time I met her, we had spent fifty years together. She was one very special lady and the love of my life.

Midge's Eulogy

My son, John, did a beautiful eulogy at the church that captured Midge's spirit for life. He said, Jenny, one of the Hospice nurses explained…Midge didn't just live life, she took it by the throat and made things happen "her way." He also said he learned about our love when we danced. We became one person gliding over the dance floor anticipating every move and gesture, completely at ease with each other.

Chapter Fourteen

Bone Cancer

Another true story of how a dramatic Second Opinion made a life changing difference for a patient with bone cancer

MY MOTHER...PAULINA JOHNSON

In her active life of over 83 years before her cancer, my mother was a very healthy, loving person to all her family and friends in both Michigan and Florida. My father had passed away years before and during this time she had learned to be very independent and that was important to her for enjoying life.

Unknown Angels

At times when we are poised for pain
the Lord seems to surround us
in ways we'll never understand
he sometimes can astound us.

From folks we've never met
or even heard their name
He's carefully selected them
to set us free from pain.

—Jack Forsberg, Jan. 2015

THE DIAGNOSIS—DEC. 2007

In late December 2007 Paulina Johnson, my mother, noticed a swelling on her right thigh. Her leg ached and she felt weary after walking. These symptoms didn't seem to go away, so she scheduled an appointment with a doctor in Sebring, Florida where she spent the winter months.

CT SCAN—JAN. 5, 2007

After the initial testing, the doctor had a CT scan performed on January 25, 2008. Approximately 10 days later, Paulina received the news of suspected chondrosarcoma, a slow growing type of bone cancer that forms in cartilage cells which is more prevalent in older people.

The doctor suggested that Paulina immediately fly back to her home state of Michigan where she had family who could assist her in locating a good hospital equipped to perform the type of surgery she would require for bone cancer.

DIAGNOSTIC RESULTS—FEB. 5, 2008

She received the news on February 5, 2008 and quickly made a call to her daughter Elaine.

Two days later I had my mother on a flight to Detroit and back to my East Lansing home. In the meantime, I had also researched numerous hospitals in the Midwestern states, making several phone calls regarding treatment facilities and physicians who would be experienced in chondrosarcoma surgery.

As it turned out, there were not many places that focused on this rare form of cancer. But, an inquiry to the University of Chicago Hospital led to a referral to the University of Michigan Hospital in Ann Arbor.

SERIES OF TESTS AND BIOPSY—FEB. 13, 2008

Paulina's first consultation appointment at U-M was on February 13, 2008 with a physician's assistant to the surgeon who performed condrosarcoma surgeries. Initial tests included an X-ray and MRI of her right femur, blood tests, and CT of the chest.

Once reviewed, a biopsy was scheduled for February 26th. The results of the biopsy would be reviewed by a team of physicians including a radiologist, oncologist and surgeon for procedural recommendations.

FIRST OPINION—MARCH 15, 2008

By mid-March Paulina had met again with the PA who told her the only surgical option would be amputation at the hip. It was explained that replacement surgery was not feasible due to the extensive nature and length of surgery required for Paulina's diagnosis, and that the particular surgery she would need to save her leg had never yet been attempted. Given her age of 83, Paulina was also told she probably could not survive such a replacement surgery. A referral to a prosthesis and rehabilitation clinic was made as the next step. Paulina had been in good health and was a very active person. Her life was about to change drastically.

DIVINE INTERVENTION? A NEW DIAGNOSIS

Her daughters and son were also trying to comprehend the situation, Then through Divine intervention, someone was placed in our presence to give another opinion. As a follow-up appointment with one of the other physicians at U-M, a door was opened. That doctor said to Paulina, "If you don't want to wait for your surgeon, I know of a very reputable surgeon located at Henry Ford Hospital in Detroit." He spoke highly of this surgeon and offered to forward all of Paulina's records to that doctor immediately if so desired. A second opinion was being considered.

SECOND OPINION—SAVED PAULINA'S LEG

After reviewing the necessary tests, Paulina's new surgeon told us that he was quite confident he could save her leg and that she could handle the procedures without endangering her life beyond typical surgical risks. He empathized the need for quality of life at Paulina's age, stating he felt if his own father were to be faced with amputation; his father would most likely lose his will to live from that moment on. The potential loss of some mobility would obviously be preferred over loss of an entire leg.

A large portion of her thigh muscle had become affected by the bone cancer, thus its removal would weaken her ability to walk after surgery. But, the surgeon performed the challenging combination of hip, femur and knee replacement with success.

SURGERY RESULTS—REHABILITATION—MORE MOBILITY

Post-surgery rehabilitation gave Paulina mobility in both legs. She was able to use a "walker" on wheels to live independently in her own home and still fly back and forth to Florida for the next four and a half years.

It was a recovery that allowed Paulina to enjoy an active life interacting with her family and friends in both Michigan and Florida.

A FAMILY PERSPECTIVE

Obviously we were all overjoyed at the success of the surgery and the rehabilitation. It allowed me and other members of our family to really get to know our mother again. These were very special years for all of us and created wonderful memories of my mother that we will never forget. The Lord works in mysterious ways and we as a family are so thankful for those extra years.

FOUR YEARS LATER: DECEMBER 2012

It wasn't until over four years later in December, 2012, that a recurrence of Paulina's cancer was discovered.

Over a two day period, a numbness in her legs turned into paralysis from her chest down due to metastasized cancer. She was given radiation treatment for a tumor on her spine, and in a pain-free, paralyzed state, Paulina passed away six weeks later on February 3, 2013. The family was grateful she didn't suffer long with the latest occurrence and thankful that the second opinion gave her four more years of mobility.

Chapter Fifteen

Major Breathing Problems

Another true story of how ignoring a patients symptoms almost cost him his life

THE FIRST SYMPTOMS—DECEMBER 2013

My name is Richard Morrow and I live in Trenton Mi and I have been a basketball coach for over 26 years. During this time I have always exercised a great deal on my own and with my teams. In December of 2013 I found I had a shortness of breath that left me feeling that something was wrong.

FIRST APPOINTMENT —DECEMBER 2, 2013

I went to Detroit Henry Ford Hospital clinic in Woodhaven Michigan. My basic test there was with my regular doctor who was an internal medicine doctor.

GENERAL ULTRASOUND TEST — DECEMBER 12, 2013

My doctor gave me a stress test and blood test and a regular check-up. From these results he recommended a cardiologist.

CARDIOLOGISTS EXAM — JANUARY 17, 2014

In January, 2014, I had an appointment with a staff cardiologist at Henry Ford Main Hospital in Detroit, Michigan

They performed a stress test with chemical evaluation, EKG, and I was observed by their cardiologist. The stress test was normal and the EKG was normal. He felt they could not find anything of concern. I went home wondering, "what was my problem? Right after I got home I noticed I still had the same shortness of breath while I was exercising and working out with my team.

STRESS TEST — MARCH 7, 2014

In March, I contacted my doctor again and he suggested that I have my annual physical which included the normal EKG and blood work, Lipid Profile, Metabolic Profile, PSA, Hemoglobin A/C BUN/ Creatinine Senun Stress Test and CT Scan, cholesterol check and other standard tests. Results normal.

When I went home and started working out again I noticed that my shortness of breath was getting worse. During this time my wife and I went on our standard vacation to my folks in Florida. I noticed during my daily run, my shortness of breath was still getting worse.

PULMONOLOGIST — MAY 5, 2014

Right after I returned from vacation I went to my cardiologist that my doctor had recommended and he sent me to a pulmonologist on staff at Ford Main Hospital in Detroit. They performed a Pulmonary Function Test. Results normal.

MAY 15, 2014

A short time later also at Henry Ford I had a DETC Plum Lab CPX. The results were compiled by their Pulmonologist. Results normal.

JUNE 3, 2014

I had a cardiopolmanary Exercise Test at HFM. Results normal

MORE TESTS—JUNE 20, 2014

My first appointment with the pulmonologist was in May, right after I returned from vacation. I went to a cardiologist that my doctor had recommended and he sent me to a pulmonologist on staff at Ford Main Hospital in Detroit. They performed a series of breathing tests. The results were compiled by their staff and presented to me around June 20th of 2014.

They asked me and my wife to come to their offices. Ther Pulmonologist asked me and my wife if I believed in Jesus, If so I was committing a sin because of my anxiety. My condition was only in my head. I was dumb founded to hear that diagnosis.

FIRST OPINION — GO HOME AND PUSH YOURSELF

He said to go home and live your life and push yourself.... meaning more exercise I went home and continued to work out as normal, still short of breath but trying harder to relax and avoid any anxiety or stress.

THE HEART ATTACK — JULY 4, 2014

A few weeks later, on July 4, I had a heart attack. My wife drove me to Henry Ford Hospital to a doctor from Brownstown Henry Ford that saved my life. He recorded the test results and sent me to the cardiac ward at Henry Ford Main in Detroit. My enzyme level did not support my heart attack. My enczyme level was at 31 and evidence of a heart attack should be 33 or above he said.

SECOND OPINION — BLOCKED ARTERY—JULY 6, 2014

I had a heart cauterization performed on July 6 in which two stents were placed in one artery. The Cardiologist said that artery was 99% blocked.

If it had closed completely, it would have been a very different result. He said, "The number one outcome of this type of blockage is death".

Anger was my first reaction. I had told my story to many doctors but because their tests didn't support my symptoms they simply just ignored my constant complaining of shortness of breath. I felt the heart attack was always going to happen….nothing was done to remedy the problem. I was very fortunate I didn't die. Even my doctor agreed with me on that.

NEW HEART TEST—SEPTEMBER, 2014

I set up an appointment to meet a new doctor in early Sept. 2014. I met the new Cardiologist at his private practice in Flat Rock, Mi. He sent me to Southshore Hospital in Trenton, Michigan where he recommended a heart imaging Neuclear test to determine any damage there was to my heart after the implants.

THE THIRD OPINION (AFTER THE STENTS)

The results were that the heart attack and implants did not damage the heart muscle or the heart valves. I was very lucky and I was put on heart meds that he prescribed for the rest of the year. I have had no other problems since my implants.

Naturally I firmly recommend another opinion … until you find a real cure for your problem. It may save your life. This is my story written shortly after it happened to me.

An Overview

ON SECOND OPINION

All of these true life stories were told by the patients or a close relative that was with the patient during all these events. There is no intention to put down any particular doctor or hospital.

The stories are presented to emphasis the fact that in many cases it may be very important to get additional opinions as to the very best type of treatment for your problem or that of a friend...whether it is cancer or some other major malady.

The health care field is a fast paced, busy environment that utilizes many people in many professions to try and find a cure for their patients. In most cases they do an excellent job. Some doctors and some hospital's may have more expertise in certain diseases than others...it is a fact of life that most would agree upon. The best advice is do your own research and compare... like you would on any other very important decision.

Hospice

When my wife first realized that her incurable lung disease gave her only a short time to live, we contacted Hospice in Grand Rapids Michigan.

At that time she was in Blake Hospital in Bradenton Florida. I arranged for a medical plane to fly her to the hospital in Grand Rapids.

Hospice arranged for a number of services for my wife Midge as soon as we reached GR.

They were very helpful in dealing with all the things that happened during this critical time.

After Midge was transported to our log home near Tustin, Michigan, Hospice came over from Evart and Big Rapids to lend a hand with all the equipment and special items needed at that time. They were especially helpful with my family and provided a source of information that helped in many ways to make it easier in a very difficult situation. I am very thankful for their help. Later they also visited me and my family.

—**Thank You**

Chapter Sixteen

Poems & Memories

A COLLECTION OF POEMS

The following Poems were inspired and written during this period of my wife's illness and afterwards while all of her memories were fresh on my mind. I hope you find some comfort in memories that may have happened to you or a loved one.

The Morning After

It's a dark grey day
with drizzling rain
and my heart aches
in ways I can't explain

like half of my body's
been torn apart
and I'm left
with the wounds
of a shattered heart

I made your coffee
to wake you dear
you were always
so lovely

just lying there
with your
satin smooth skin
and your tousled hair
It was like you
are in a state of grace
such a peaceful pose
how I loved that face

I placed your coffee
beside our bed
and after you'd slept awhile
I said, there's not one wrinkle
in that beautiful face
they've all gone away
it seems
and you would say
in your usual way
yeah…only in your dreams

But now I reach out
and you're not there
the empty pillow is all
and the tears are back
like the morning rain
and good times are hard to recall

Then my body shakes
with this terrible ache
and tears come
in a flood of pain
and the silence is broken
by my own voice
as I hear me

calling your name
Then I'm up
and look in the mirror
I'm a mess from my morning cry
and I ask again
that same question
Oh Midge…..Why did you have to die?

I had asked you
to find a way
so I knew you were alright
some simple thing
your spirit could do
like turning on a light

My knee massager
wouldn't work
the batteries must be dead
I'll put it on the counter
and try it later is what I said

I was shuffling around
in my crying state
asking the question…whjy?

when the movement
of my knee massager
caught my eye
it was buzzing loudly
doing circles
on the counter space nearby.

—Jack Forsberg…As it happened, May 20, 2014

The Journey Alone

Before my wife passed away
in those very final days
I knew I would be
one very lonesome soul
But now I find
I am learning how
the real loss takes its toll

No, its' not what I expected
It's like my body's been dissected
half my life's been swept away
and I'm finding every day
that my memories
can't replace this awful void

In the space of fifty years
through the laughter
and the tears
we celebrated
the commotions of a life
and I was fortunate
to find one that always
read my mind
and that was Midge
my ever loving wife

Now my life has not just changed
its been totally rearranged
into a singular perspective
that is foreign to my soul

I no longer have confirmation
of any situation
I'm left drifting in a current
going where?

I'm a former alpha male
carrying on without a sail
No compass seems to help
to point the way
there's no wind or water
in this empty bay.

— Jack Forsberg, Sept. 2014

God's Special Angels

The Lord has these special angels
that he sprinkled on this earth
like gold dust for his people
he has nurtured them
from birth

There is no explanation
for the things they daily do
But all of those they comfort
find a sense of life renewed

The peace of mind
that they bestow
seems to come from
God's own hand
and goes beyond
our mortal minds
to try and understand

The ability to listen
is built into their genes
they learn to love
the one you've lost
like a road map
to your dreams

You would think
the sorrow they consume
would wound them in this role

But instead it ignites
the joy of life
adding love to every soul

So I thank God's
special angels
for dopping by today
to re-live
precious memories
of a love
just passed away.

     —Jack Forsberg, Sept. 5, 2014

The Chaplain

Some morning's Lord
I seek you out
looking for a word in vain
a word to set me on a path
some path you could explain

This morning Lord
I found that word
within my private mantel
A pathway I must follow now
to light a Chaplains channel

Providing a pathway to cope
for someone
that really needs that hope

Someone like me and my wife
a few year ago
when I felt we had
no way to go

But a Chaplain
helped us find a way
to turn our lives around
as we were shown
the power of God
in a way I found profound

It's hard to explain
how weeks of pain
could just disappear
but it's a story
I would tell you
if you were sitting here

But it was months
before that happened
and that is the story
I must tell
Before God changed our life
We went through
our private hell.

—Jack Forsberg, Oct. 2014

Let Her Live Lord

When the strongest
of our loved ones
break down to you in tears
and the pain
is so unyielding
we can feel the end is near

Then your love's
our only anchor
on this fragile ship of life,
and I feel
my life receding
as your reaching
for my wife.

The power of your love
is so much stronger
than my own
 I know I"ll lose the battle
if you choose
to call her home,

I know only our prayers
can change this rising tide
So I pray you let me keep her
for awhile…by my side.

—Jack Forsberg, Feb., 2010

The Stone

The sight of it grabs
your breath and
cuts you to the bone
you've never…ever
felt as bad
as staring at that stone

The words are there
 for all to stare
the very day she died
it cuts out
every shred of hope
that both of us had tried

This cemetery used to be
fond memories…
close to home
now its nothing but
that one sad site
Oh God, I feel alone

The end of fifty years
of love
are buried neath that stone
plus everything
that could have been
Oh God…I am so alone

Like all the things
we did together
all the things we tried.
our names will be forever linked
for years after I die

And years from now
when I am there
in that same resting place
the memories that we shared
may bring a smile
to an old friends face

But today there are
no smiles, no friends
to share the pain
no more false hopes
that we could cope
with things
they can't explain
and only here
under our stone
were you finally free from pain.

Five special kind of flowers
each one a different hue
like your garden at the cabin
each reminded me of you.

—Jack Forsberg, July, 2014

Memories

I'm a man heading
for a distant shore
but there's no one pulling
on that other oar

there's no smile in the morning
when the coffee's done
no one to ask about
our daughter or son's

She'd go shopping
but not just for herself
I'd have a new thing to wear
or to put on the shelf

My friends tell me
this time will pass
but right now
I want to remember the past

like sharing the wonders
of a waterfall
or seeing the flowers
she planted last fall

I like how she always
read my mind
pointed out things
I couldn't find

Now her pain's gone
she's finally at rest
She passed every challenge
God gave her to test

Together we designed her stone
But it's a tough thing to share
when you stand here alone.

—Jack Forsberg, July 29, 2014

Love

No matter how hard
your life may be
it's the power of love
that sets you free

From one small room
to a cathedral in Rome
love is the joy
that turns it into a home

The Lord started heaven
with a single goal
to put love
into every human soul

The melody of love
is to bring you joy
it's there in the heart
of every girl and boy

From the darkest prison
to the mountain peaks
Love is the answer
that our hearts all seek

You can hear it in the music
of our melodies
whether we sing for joy
or were on our knees

It's the Lord's own music
that he's put in our hearts
It brings us all together
when were falling apart

Yes the Lord started heaven
with a single goal
to put his love into every soul

It's that heavenly music
that the angel's sing
it's your reminder
that he loves all things

He loves each of us
despite our feet of clay
and that heavenly music
helps to point the way

When you hear that music
with a joyful roll
You can see the Lord smiling
 on another soul

He loves your spirit
and he loves your fire
One day you'll be part
of his heavenly choir.

—Jack Forsberg, Jan., 2015

My Cancer

Like an alien being
that sight unseen
started growing
inside of my bod,
from where it came
I don't know
but it continues to grow
and it has nothing to do
with my God

It spirals around
like a worm unwound
and challenges us
to undo it,
the doctors feel sure
they have a real cure
if they do
I sure wish they would do it.

They test trial things
that continually brings
side effects that can
drive you quite mad,
from the nauseous and pain
the doctors explain
we don't know
why it's really that bad

It only seems fair
as I'm losing my hair
that my doctor
should be by my side,

Watch his grin
turn to grim,
as it happens to him
now he's not
just along for the ride,

The answers may be
in some foreign tree
in a jungle
we've yet to explore
a poisonous drug
that would capture this bug
and leave me as I was before,

But if being too nice
just doesn't cut the ice
then let the bug
be devoured with glee
let the cancer;'s demise
be a joy to my eyes
as I watch that thing suffer…like me.

— Jack Forsberg, Dec., 2009

To Understand God's Love

Breathe in me the sea of love
from which all things must flow
with my hands shape the gentleness
that constitutes His soul.

For if unto me His will be given
to recreate His love
I'd spend a year in solitude
before I touched a brush.

And as His understanding love
cleft down my human fallacies
I find myself less quick to judge
more often on my knees.

I stand in naked ignorance
before eternity
so place your hand upon my heart
and let me know of Thee

— Jack Forsberg 1965

The Exchange

I awoke one morning to
an empty page of life
and exchanged the peace of Jesus
for the grief of my wife

The love I will remember
is still in my memories
but the terrible grief and sorrow
have somehow been set free..

—Jack Forsberg, April 1, 2015

The Anniversary

We celebrate the good times
with relatives and friends
and give a toast to anniversaries
and hope they never end

But some friends I've met
just can't forget
that certain special day…
that day that really changed their life
in Oh, so many ways

Their struggle with the doctors
prescriptions and the tests
searching for that miracle
and hoping for the best

It's hard to explain
the late night pains
the hospitals at night
the doctors and the nurses
sometime's are wound up tight

The shootings and the drugs
puts pressure on two fold
they're too busy with all of this
than patients…that are old

But life goes on
and all things end

no matter how hard the task
to share their grief
brings some relief
is usually all they ask

So I remember my special day
my anniversary in May
it was just two months ago today
that my wife Midge passed away

The anniversary remains
one day I never can explain
a scar so swift it wiped away
a half a lifetime in a day

Memories ingrained so deep
I know I will forever keep
them locked away
in my private trust
so they will never fade or rust

Sometime when the time is right
I will take them out at night
and re-live those times from years ago
when our love was all that mattered so

When that anniversary
does not bring tears
but only pleasant memories
from all those special years

—Jack Forsberg, August 2014

Leave It Behind

There's too many things
we find on our mind
We'd be better off
if we left them behind

 Lets make it a mandate
to separate
some things from the past
and just keep the good parts
we know that will last

Lets push those
old jealousies
way back behind
and throw those old hatreds
right out of our mind

The bad words we heard
about a friend when he died
has nothing to do
with the great things he tried

Those folks that we met
from a whole different race
sure made a big difference
sprucing up that old place

I feel kinda bad
never saying 'hello"
they seemed like folks
I should get to know

Like Jesus told John
when they met on the shore
leave your boat and your nets
you won't need them no more

There are so many burdens
we keep carrying inside
It would lighten our load
if we set them aside

Once they're gone
its much easier to see
what's really important
from the things we don't need

So lets live with the promise
to clean up our mind
and remember our friends
and the good things we find

As we leave that old stuff
behind us
it lightens our load
And we"ll discover new joy
on God's easier road,

—Jack Forsberg, August 2014

The Vatican

We were finally in
 the Vatican
We climbed those holy stairs
and thanked the Lord
for Midge's life
during our Sunday Prayers

The beauty there was so intense
like the lord's own resting place
the communion and
the choir put you in a state of grace

The joy that followed
us that day is so hard to explain
Like sunlight surrounded us
and swept away the rain

Some mornings now
when I am near to tears
I see that holy place again
it's majesty appears
and I thank the Lord
for that extra time ...
those very special years

Time goes by so quickly
when the race is being run
we seldom take the time
to share each other's fun

The saddest words I ever heard
by someone just gone lame
Oh how I wished we hadn't missed
our chance to go to Spain.

You never know
what's just ahead
and how your life may twist
so you may want to take a pen
and start *your* 'bucket List.".

—Jack Forsberg, Sept. 2014

Song Of The Loons

I watched as the geese
were gathering
listening to their calls
in the night
beckoning me to join them
in the wondrous
freedom of flight

The Monarchs are back
to the Lilac bush they prefer
Over thousands of miles
they have winged it
still just the same as they were.

The lightening quick flash
of a humming birds wings
surprises my eyes
to its flight
how it can appear
and disappear
is a mystery that
always delights

Poking my toes
in the white sand
watching the Egrets in flight
searching for shells
in the new surf
laughing as kids fly their kites

Wandering with the wind
where it leads me
catching the mist from the rain
listening to the
distant thunder
feeling more alive than I can explain.

Watching her eyes
as they come alive
seeing the cardinals are here
they are back
to their home on the Pine
like us
for another year.

Our love's like the
song of the loons
a beautiful sound in the night
at the first light of dawn
you can watch them fly on
always together in flight.

—Jack Forsberg, June 10, 2013

Midge

There are people that help shape our lives
and add a smile to our days
Midge had that gift
for lifting you up
In a hundred little ways

A log home became her compulsion
the Pine River part of the lure
so I designed and we built it
especially for her

Midge chose every piece of the puzzle
and helped to stain every log
And between Midge, John and I
We did it…or tried
and worked like a good team of dogs.

She held up every stone in the fireplace
and we told her where it should go
but if she didn't agree,, She did it her way
and told us where we could go

As I remember we started in September
And finished it off early spring
Before long she was seeing new fawns
And young turkeys were testing their wings

I caught fresh trout from the river
and Midge fried them up in a pan
it doesn't get any better than that
for Jack or any man.

Then cancer suddenly
threatened Midge
And some doctors made it worse
But with God's help Midge fought it
And put cancer into reverse

The good thing though, Midge now knows
Her many Tustin friends
Thru all of her grief
she found relief
in their prayers and amens

Although our kids are all grown up
they've stayed close to mother hen

it's not a question if they called
but if she hadn't heard at all
she's asking what, why and when?

For years we made a bucket list
on what Midge would like to see
So on Holland America
we sailed the seven seas

For many years Midge was Catholic
but shared the Lutheran faith with me
She said this Lutheran Church in Tustin
was a joyful place to be

The highlight of our trips
was the Vatican in Rome
We had high mass on Sunday
in the very same place
The Catholic Pope calls home

I got to see Michelangelo's paintings
and Rafellos's paintings too
and Midge saw 500 years ago
they were wearing her summer shoes

When we came home Midge
edited and published
three special books for me
plus a poetry book for my brother
for all his friends to see

Then the side effects of cancer
returned with a crushing blow
And nothing we could do
would stop it
as sadly we now know

But your cards and letters
made Midge feel better
She knew she had friends that cared
she always told me
to thank each one
because those kind of friends
are rare

So after fifty years of
laughter and tears
I feel I know for sure
She was one of Gods special people
and I took good care of her

There is no doubt by anyone
no matter who they may be
That she was the focus of my life
and she took better care of me

Thanks Midge for
a Wonderful Life

—Jack Forsberg, Oct. 2014

The Last Day

The day I finished this book with all the changes indicated for final printing...it got very, very dark outside like it was late at night. I had the feeling it reflected my mood at the end of a long tunnel of dark work reliving Midge's death and passing and the final work on the book with all its really sad moments of both our lives.

I wonder how the book will be received. It is both a dark story of pain and suffering and a story of hope and joyful recovery...but more pain and how it can continue even after you think you have put cancer into remission. It is very dark and very quiet, not a leaf is moving...the rain has stopped.

I just hope it helps save some lives...Midge would have wanted that.

Special Thanks

To Ruth Hammar for her sunset photo of Anna Maria Island, Florida that she graciously permitted me to use on the cover.

To John Forsberg for his terrific cover design.

To Mary Raven, Jane Siglin and Ruth Hammar, my steadfast editors and proofreaders.

To Ron Gries and Marie Mallone, RN, BSN for both editing and valuable moral support through many months of work on this book.

—Jack

Questions To Ask Your Doctor or Hospital Oncologist

From my test RESULTS can you tell me.

1. What type of cancer do I have?
   Is it a virus, a bacteria, is it hereditary or could it be caused from the environment? Is it fast growth or slow growth?

2. What are my options for Treatment?
   Chemo, Radiation, Surgery or what other?

3. For my type of cancer, are there proven methods of treatment that can put it into remission?

4. Are you associated with test trial programs or are you affiliated with Cancer Research Centers?

5. If I agree to have Chemo, how effective are the drugs to prevent nausea and hair loss? How long would the chemo normally take to put my cancer into remission? Times for other treatments?

6. Are you aware of another facility that might be a better fit for curing my type of cancer? Would you advise a second opinion at this point?

7. There are so many unknown factors. Could you just offer me the ultimate known and tested program available?

8. What is most beneficial...to increase my activity, moderate or more rest? Is there anything I should be very concerned about, or to avoid before treatment?.

Other Books By The Author

Fireflys and Dynamite

A book of stories growing up in the 30's and 40's during the depression and WW II. Includes a wide variety of experiences, some joyful and humorous and some strange and terrible to a young boy growing up in these violent times. Includes unusual hunting experiences at a time when hunting was also putting food on the table.

Beat The Anvil

A book of poems based on happenings the author experienced in traveling around the country. Things that were of special interest and made a deep impression on him. A book of poems that highlights the beauty of this country and the importance of friendships and love in our daily lives, the opposite of today's news.

2500 Miles in a Tank

The experiences of Bill Hammar during WWII as he drove a tank all the way from the southern tip of France across that nation and all the way across Germany and into Austria. Includes both the day to day life with a tank commander and the violent acts of war their tanks were exposed to during this time as they were rushing to the final solution of WWII. Bill Hammar was a long time resident of Tustin, Michigan.

Midge and Jack at Bond Falls in the Upper Pennisula

About The Author

I went to Central Michigan College in Mt. Pleasant Michigan. A year later I transferred to Kendal School of Design in Grand Rapids and graduated in graphic design. I got the idea of recording my thoughts in poems whereever I traveled and I have done this my entire life. My wife and I started our own Ad Agency called Forsberg Advertising in Lansing, Michigan. Midge was always an important part of it becoming comptroller of the firm as it grew over a forty year period. I wrote articles for our clients that were placed in national trade magazine. My wife edited and proofed all of my articles. Upon retirement, I wrote three books which Midge edited and published.